MW00604173

Book Review by Ronald Moss
(School administrator and avid whitetail hunter)

I've been hunting the whitetail for 38 years. I was fortunate to have a grandfather, uncles, and older brothers to teach me the arts/skills of the sport and have continued to study the whitetail ever since. I started hunting the whitetail with the author of *SKILLFULLY HUNTING THE ELUSIVE WHITETAIL,* Mr. Woods, in 1978 and like to think that I contributed to the wealth of knowledge contained in this book. The author has a passion for the sport and approaches whitetail hunting in a methodical/analytical manner. We both have primarily used the bow as our shooting device, which accentuates the need to maximize hunting skills. *SKILLFULLY HUNTING THE ELUSIVE WHITETAIL* clearly illustrates that Mr. Woods has mastered the art/science of hunting the whitetail. I highly recommend this book to anyone wanting to learn the sport of hunting the whitetail. Every paragraph teaches a specific point. There are no long-winded, egocentric, self-serving stories in this book. Even the photographs contribute to making his points. You'll be glad that you spent a couple of hours reading it.

Book Review by Becky Bull
(Schoolteacher & avid nature enthusiast)

As an avid nature enthusiast (a.k.a. "Bambi" lover), I may have had some subconscious prejudices before reading Mr. Woods' *SKILLFULLY HUNTING THE ELUSIVE WHITETAIL.* After reading it however, I can truly say I was very impressed. Mr. Woods not only treats the skill/art of hunting with great respect but also demonstrates and encourages a great respect for nature. This book is not only a 'how-to-hunt' book but is also a study in good sportsmanship. The apparent field research and data collected by Mr. Woods on the whitetail deer give evidence of Mr. Woods' extensive knowledge and authority on the subject, which as a reader, I found to be quite impressive. I also appreciated the humorous side of Mr. Woods' personality. I believe that anyone using this book as a 'how-to-manual' would become a successful hunter, and also develop a great deal of self-respect along the way. This is definitely the ultimate SURVIVOR book.

Book Review by Brian Mullins
(Veteran Whitetail Hunter of 15 Years)

I've been a dedicated whitetail hunter for the past 15 years. I love the sport and have spent countless hours studying the whitetail in its natural habitat as well as reading any books and magazine articles that I thought may teach me something about hunting the whitetail that I did not already know. *SGKILLFULLY HUNTING THE ELUSIVE WHITETAIL* cuts-to-the-chaff and tells whitetail hunters, or people considering the sport, what they need to know to be effective in the woods. The huge majority of people that I've known, who call themselves whitetail hunters, are not hunters at all. They are what Mr. Woods calls "Luck Hunters". These people may kill a deer once in a great while, but if they took the time to read this book, they could quickly learn the basics of the sport. Most books/articles that I've read only deal with a small part of whitetail hunting. They normally belabor unimportant points. They frequently are riddled with poor advice, seemingly based on one or two experiences or parroting what some guide may have tried to impress them with. Mr. Woods' book is accurate and is more complete than any other book that I can remember. I strongly recommend Mr. Woods' book to anyone wanting to learn the sport or wanting to refine his or her hunting skills.

SKILLFULLY HUNTING THE ELUSIVE WHITETAIL

Table of Contents

- ❖ Preface/Introduction — 6
- ❖ Chapter One - Getting to Know the Whitetail Deer — 7
  - ➢ Whitetail's Vulnerabilities - Food and Sex — 8
  - ➢ Whitetail's Defenses - Smell, Hearing, and Sight — 20
- ❖ Chapter Two - When Whitetail Move Most — 23
  - ➢ Seasons Impact — 23
  - ➢ Time of Day Impact — 24
  - ➢ Weather Impact — 25
  - ➢ Moon Impact — 27
  - ➢ Summary of When Whitetail Move Most — 28
- ❖ Chapter Three - Selecting an Area to Hunt — 29
  - ➢ State/County/Area to Hunt — 29
  - ➢ Public vs. Private Land — 30
- ❖ Chapter Four - Overview of Methods to Harvesting Whitetail — 36
- ❖ Chapter Five - Stand Hunting - Picking Stand Locations — 39
  - ➢ Travel Pattern — 39
  - ➢ Funneling Them to You — 42
  - ➢ Reading Sign — 46
  - ➢ Scouting — 50
  - ➢ Unfamiliar Areas — 51
  - ➢ Controlling Your Scent Trail — 52
  - ➢ Picking Tree for Portable Tree Stand — 53
  - ➢ Permanent Tree Stands — 54
  - ➢ Picking Your Ground Blind Location — 55
- ❖ Chapter Six - Stand Hunting - Getting to Your Stand — 56
  - ➢ From Bed to Hunting Area — 56
  - ➢ From Vehicle to Stand — 56
  - ➢ When You Get to Your Stand — 57
- ❖ Chapter Seven - Stand Hunting - At Your Stand — 58
  - ➢ Scent Control — 58
  - ➢ Sound Control — 59
  - ➢ Sight Control — 59
  - ➢ Change Stands Frequently — 61
  - ➢ Talking to Trophy Bucks (Deer Calling Techniques) — 61
  - ➢ At Your Stand Pointers — 68
- ❖ Chapter Eight - Other Hunting Methods — 73
  - ➢ Still Hunting — 73
  - ➢ Drive Hunting — 75
  - ➢ Boat Hunting — 75
- ❖ Chapter Nine - Hunting Trophy Bucks — 77
- ❖ Chapter Ten - After You Shoot — 81
  - ➢ Tracking Wounded Deer — 81
  - ➢ After You Find Your Deer — 82

❖ Chapter Eleven - Butchering Your Deer   85
    ➢ Skin and Quarter   85
    ➢ Prepare Venison for Freezer   86
❖ Chapter Twelve – Equipment   87
    ➢ Compound Bow/Crossbow   87
    ➢ Gun   89
    ➢ Muzzleloader   91
    ➢ Pistols   93
    ➢ Shotgun   93
    ➢ Scopes   94
    ➢ Sight-In   94
    ➢ Portable Tree Stand   94
    ➢ Ground Blind   96
    ➢ Tree Umbrella   96
    ➢ Deer Calls   96
    ➢ Vehicle Gear   97
    ➢ Luxury Equipment   97
❖ Chapter Thirteen – Clothing   99
    ➢ Utility Belt, Satchel or Utility Vest?   99
    ➢ Warm Weather - Bow Season   100
    ➢ Cold Weather - Gun Season   101
❖ Chapter Fourteen - Whitetail Hunting Safety   103
❖ Chapter Fifteen - Persistence   105
❖ Appendix - Whitetail Data by State   107

SKILLFULLY HUNTING THE ELUSIVE WHITETAIL

Preface/Introduction

The objective of this book is to provide the reader with an accurate and to-the-point learning tool, and all of the knowledge required to become a highly skilled whitetail hunter. For the beginning whitetail hunter, it will get you started hunting the whitetail deer without wasting years learning by trial and error. For the hunter with significant experience, it should make you a better hunter rather quickly. For the long time serious whitetail hunter it should (1) give you a few new points to think about, (2) reinforce what you already know, (3) remind you of points that you have forgotten and/or (4) in those cases where you may disagree with my points, make you rethink your logic.

This book is an attempt to bring the significant points of whitetail hunting under one cover and to present it to you in a brief, to-the-point manner. This is why I chose the modified outline style of writing. You should not have to read pages and pages in this book to learn new points. This style of writing should also allow you to review points that you want to "brush-up on" rather quickly. If you are looking for a book full of jokes, and insignificant deer hunting stories, this book is not for you. If you want to read a blow-by-blow account of a two-year deer research study, this book is not for you. On the other hand, if you want to quickly learn the basics of whitetail hunting, you will be glad that you read this book.

To make this book the most accurate and complete whitetail-hunting guide in print today, I selected three of the best trophy whitetail deer hunters that I know, to read and critique the book. They all agreed with the points that I included. Two added some points that I had not thought of or used in my hunting career. These points are included in this book. These superior hunters rated this book as excellent or outstanding in the areas of reality and accuracy.

This book is dedicated to those people, thirteen years old or sixty, who like myself, were not so lucky to have had a mentor to teach them how to become a highly skilled whitetail deer hunter. It is also dedicated to anyone who loves the woods as much as I. Lastly, it is dedicated to the most fascinating animal that I've ever known – the Whitetail Deer.

If you are a turkey hunter (or would like to learn to hunt the wild turkey) you may be interested in reading my book, *SKILLFULLY HUNTING THE KEEN-EYED WILD TURKEY*. This book brings all significant points of turkey hunting under one cover and is presented in a brief, to-the-point manner.

Chapter One
Get to Know the Whitetail Deer

The most important prerequisite to becoming a proficient whitetail deer hunter is to learn and understand the whitetail's vulnerabilities, defenses, social behavior, food supply and preferences, travel patterns, and their communication system. Mastering this knowledge will help you to: (1) analyze potential hunting spots, (2) formulate a plan/strategy to "outsmart" the whitetail's instincts, and (3) prevent you from underestimating your adversary. Whitetail hunting is a sport of exceptions. Within this book, I try to give the reader the "most-of-the time" rules as well as some of the exceptions to the "rules". Whitetail hunting is an art, meaning it is not a science; rather, it requires exercising intuitive judgments that cannot be learned solely by study. To become proficient at this art requires the hunter to learn many new skills and then practice applying them in the deer woods. The more that a hunter is willing to learn and practice, the more successful they will become. Some people call harvesting whitetail luck; and, indeed, it is for that hunter who has no hunting skills. But, for a highly skilled whitetail hunter harvesting a deer is not luck. The probability formulas of statistics say that the more things that a hunter does correctly in the woods, the higher the probability that the hunter will be dragging a deer when he comes out of the woods.

The more a hunter knows about the whitetail, the faster that hunter is able to accurately predict where/when the deer will be traveling. Rather than guessing at how the deer are moving and when they will be at a certain spot before finally making contact. Trial and error wastes hunting time. Even after locating the perfect spot to harvest a deer, the hunter could waste additional hunting time (or spook them to relocating) if the setup stand is incorrectly selected. Again, trial and error wastes hunting time. Furthermore, few plans work exactly as formulated. It is difficult to premeditate a whitetail hunting strategy, and then follow through exactly as planned. The elusive whitetail almost always does something unexpected. It is necessary, then, to know how the whitetail normally responds to different situations. This allows the hunter to alter their original plan as the whitetail deviates from the original expectations. By learning some general guidelines, it will allow the hunter to respond a little faster and a little more accurately, even under pressure.

When the Allies liberated Kuwait, during operation Desert Storm in 1991, we didn't simply pull our ships in and attack. The Allies knew Iraq's strong points and weak points. We knew where their supply lines, ammunition and food dumps, communication centers, and other strategic targets were. We probably knew what the troops had for breakfast and where they went to get it. In short, the Allied forces knew Iraq's vulnerabilities and defenses and formulated a strategy to take advantage of both. The result was a total victory in just a few days. Whitetail hunting is no different. If you simply "attack" the whitetail, not knowing their vulnerabilities and defenses and have no plan, or a plan based on erroneous information, the whitetail will win the battle. You'll probably come out of the woods with a wounded pride and be empty-handed.

Only about one out of 2.2 hunters, buying a whitetail permit, fill even one kill tag per season. This number is based on data from fifteen states, including over four and one quarter million whitetail hunters. This fact is no coincidence. The whitetail deer (odocoileus virginianus) is not a highly intelligent animal but God did grace them with excellent instincts. So, why does only one out of 2.2 whitetail hunters make a kill for a given season? The answer is simple. Most whitetail hunters have not bothered to learn/understand their adversary's vulnerabilities and defenses. They don't do enough reconnaissance (scouting) to determine where the whitetail's supply lines (trails), headquarters (bedding areas) or food dumps (primary/secondary feeding) are located. Nor do they bother learning their communication system (calling/rattling). If the Allies had approached Desert Storm the way most whitetail hunters approach hunting, would we have won the war?

- ❖ Whitetail's Vulnerabilities - Food and Sex
  - ➢ Food - The life of a whitetail revolves around its stomach. Depending on its size, a whitetail will consume ten to twenty pounds of forage to fill its paunch. They normally make an effort to fill their paunch twice per day, which requires considerable browsing/moving. They feed heavily from predawn until an hour or so after daylight. They then find a comfortable resting spot in good cover and lie down. They'll get up occasionally and feed a bit in or around their bedding area of good cover and lie down again, probably in a different location. At late afternoon, they'll get up and feed seriously again. Harvest studies show that as many as ninety percent of whitetails bagged, availed themselves to hunters, because they were moving and exposing themselves during daylight hours. The whitetail must move to fill their paunch, and the scarcer the food supply, the more moving they have to do and the more vulnerable they become to the hunter.

Deer will adapt to eating a very wide variety of foods. This is why they exist in such a vast variety of climates and areas. Food sources vary dramatically from state to state and even county to county and I can't begin to give you a list of all of them. Rather, I will give you examples of what you should look for in your hunting area. Learn what deer love to eat and which of these foods are in your hunting area. Acorns are one of their favorite and don't forget it. There are many types of oak trees. Deer prefer acorns from some oaks to others. Acorns from the white oak, pin oaks, and live oaks are among their favorites, and are among the first to start falling. It's difficult to learn all of the different oaks; so, a general rule of thumb is that the bigger the acorn, the less the deer prefer them. After a freeze or two they begin to eat the larger acorns, especially chestnut oaks. By then, their more favorite acorns are probably getting harder to find, and the larger acorns become more palatable to the whitetail. Beechnuts, chestnuts, pecans, and buckeyes are in a high preference class, but are rather unusual finds in areas that I have hunted. Farmer's soybeans, clover, alfalfa, greens, collards, buckwheat, corn, sorghum, winter wheat/oats, etc. are a high preference and high volume staples deer will travel miles to use. Farmer's regular fescue/rye/timothy grass pasture/hay fields are also sought by the whitetails, especially if they are newly sewn. Honeysuckle; cane from cane breaks; pine tops; maple, birch, aspen, sumac, and poplar new growth; etc. are high volume staples they can normally count on to fill their paunch. Whitetail can smell mushrooms inches under the leaves/pine-needles and will dig them out if they have to. Muscadines (in early bow season) and honey locust fruit (gun season) also grow wild in some hunting areas. Deer's preference for these depends on alternative foods available at the time. Personally, I've not seen much evidence of deer being too crazy about them. It's not often that you find an apple or pear tree in a wooded area; but, occasionally you do in old home places, and deer love both fruits. Crab apples, persimmons, and hedge apples (looks like a grapefruit) grow wild in some hunting areas. They start eating crab apples as they fall during bow season. They prefer persimmons after the first good frost. They don't like hedge apples until they have lain on the ground until they become ripe, which will be after mid November. Huajillo, pinons, sage, manzanita, and bitterbrush are some favorites in western states. Plant food plots to attract deer to the area. Plant clover, alfalfa, timothy, greens, winter wheat, oats, buckwheat, chufa, sorghum, beans, soybeans, peas, etc. If you want to do it once and hope that it lasts for years, plant clover, alfalfa, timothy, etc. Try to time an annual crop so it will be ready when you can hunt. Place salt near/in heavy cover, somewhere around a food plot, but make sure that you place it near major trails. Dig out a few inches of soil and pour loose salt in the hole, mixing it with some of the dirt that you dug out. Some hunters use mineral salt and some hunters use white salt. I use salt especially formulated for deer, which can be purchased at your farmer's Co-Op or local feed store. It has several other minerals that deer need to stay healthy and develop good racks. Once I started two wallows side by side. In one I used mineral salt ("high mag."), and in the other I used the deer salt. The deer used the deer salt wallow much more than the mineral salt wallow. Don't use block salt or rock salt. Loose salt becomes part of the soil quickly and eating soil is the deer's natural way of getting minerals. Whitetails use these wallows heavily during spring and summer, but will not use them much during the fall and winter.

Three Week Old Salt Wallow

Three Month Old Salt Wallow

Install a large feeder, like the one pictured below, and fill it with shelled corn. This will help deer through January and February, help keep deer in a particular area, and will only have to be filled about once per week. It is illegal and unsporting to hunt at these feed spots, but you can hunt the trails leading to such feeders.

Deer Feeder

Place food blocks and/or Deer Cocaine (a liquid solution with minerals and sugar) in similar spots. I use Corn-Lix Deer Block by Sweetlix LLC in Salt Lake City, Utah. It has calcium, phosphorus, salt, magnesium sulfate, magnesium oxide, zinc sulfate, zinc oxide, copper sulfate, copper iodate, vitamins A, D-3 and E, etc. and deer love it. I place the deer blocks near my salt wallow. The deer blocks are formulated to supplement the deer's natural vegetation by providing essential minerals to maximize growth, reproduction, and antler/bone development. The variables affecting a buck's rack size are food and minerals in their diet, genetics, buck/doe ratio, and the buck's age. I figure that I can control the food/mineral variable easier than the other variables. Ideally, you should keep the blocks available all year long, but this gets expensive. I use them during the barren months and while the bucks are developing new racks from about February through September. You can get a fair idea of the deer population in an area by using deer blocks. In an area with a heavy deer population, a deer block will last about two weeks. In an area with a fair to poor deer population, the deer block may last six weeks. After acorns start falling, the whitetail will ignore these blocks.

If you have a problem loading a feeder on a short interval basis, consider using time-release automatic dispensing feeders. These feeders normally are DC battery powered and allow the user to vary the time between feedings as well as the quantity dispensed at each feeding. Such dispensing systems are manufactured by: On Time Wildlife Feeders (978-449-0121), Game Country/Moultrie (888-900-4868), Kenco, Cast Wildlife Feeders (1-800-950-7087) and other companies. Since the hunter can set the exact time the feed is dispensed, the hunter may be able to alter the game's feeding pattern to better fit his hunting schedule.

Deer will not gorge themselves with one item. As much as they like acorns, they want other items in their diet. Regardless of how many acorns are on the ground, they will normally move toward the farmer's fields toward dark, and away from them in the morning, munching on acorns and whatever along the way. When you make a kill, cut the stomach open and determine what it has been eating. This will tell you what their current food sources are, and help you determine their travel patterns.

➤ Sex (The instinct of the species to reproduce) - Learn what revealing signs deer leave, when they are preoccupied with sex. A buck can service six or eight does without any trouble. This keeps him busy (and may cause him to get careless) beginning in mid October and sometimes lasting through December.

Scrapes (pawing on the ground) - Scrapes are the chief sign used by breeding bucks, and can be VERY IMPORTANT to the hunter. Most veteran hunters agree that hunting near scrapes is the best way to get within shooting range of a buck. The buck makes the scrape and urinates in it. He may chew or horn an overhanging branch to leave his signature scents. When a doe is coming into heat, she seeks these scrapes and also urinates in them. When the buck returns to the scrape, and smells the doe urine, he may start looking for that doe.

Scrape making begins about two weeks prior to the actual breeding, in mid October. Peak scrape making starts about two weeks prior to the breeding peak (sometime between late October to mid November). If an area shows scraping activity in October and the scrapes are numerous, large, and well constructed, it is probably that of a big buck. The same dominant buck normally makes scrapes in a given area. Numerous and small scrapes were likely made by a lesser buck. A dominant buck may make dozens or hundreds of scrapes each fall, but will revisit only those few that generate the most doe encounters. Some scrapes are meant only as a warning to lesser bucks, marking off a breeding area for him. Even if a scrape is one of the dominant buck's main scrapes, he may not visit it for days. He may be accompanying a doe nearing estrus. Estrus is a 24 to 36 hour period when the doe is receptive to breeding. She will come back into heat every 28 days until she is bred. Sometimes the dominant buck will check a scrape several times in one day, but may not come within a hundred yards of the scrape. The glandular scents of breeding does and bucks carry through the air for a long distance. Also, a very nocturnal buck may do all scrape checking at night.

14

Key Scrapes will usually be oval in shape, two to four feet long by one to three feet wide. The ground will be churned-up, raked mostly with hooves but sometimes with antler tines. Look for a hoof track in it and dampness from urine. You may smell the urine also. It may be under a low branch, that the buck may thrash or chew on, distributing his scent. Without this overhanging branch, the scrape may not be a serious scrape. Sometimes you'll see a scrape with a small sapling somewhere in the middle that he uses to thrash and chew on, rather than using an overhanging branch. If you cannot locate a scrape with an overhanging branch, take the best that you can find. Sometimes you'll find small scrapes in a meandering line, similar to a "rub line" (discussed below), but finding a "bunch" of large and well defined scrapes in one area will probably be more productive for the trophy hunter. Also, the more thick cover that surrounds scrapes, the more likely that a highly nocturnal buck will come to the scrapes during daylight hours.

A buck may place emphasis on a few scrapes for a week or so, and suddenly put more emphasis on another set, not far away. The dominant buck may not be the one that shows up at the scrape. Since other bucks may visit a dominant buck's scrapes, hunting over scrapes may be productive, even though the dominant buck is not visiting them at the moment. Lesser bucks may expose themselves more during daylight hours than the dominant buck. Lesser bucks will even use the dominant buck's scrapes, while the dominant buck has gone visiting. If the dominant buck catches the lesser buck at his scrape, he will chase the lesser buck away and redo his scrape.

Dominant bucks use the same area for key scrapes year after year. The buck seems to prefer edges of thick growth to make scrapes. You're also likely to find them in old logging roads, or similar openings, among the thick cover. A significant amount of open field areas means that the buck will build scrapes at the edge of these fields, under low hanging branches. Once a dominant buck is killed, the one taking his place may also use these same areas. To determine if a scrape is active, you can cover the scrape with leaves/needles (use your rubber boots to kick it in to minimize scent) and come back, say, daily to see if the scrape has been cleaned out. You can also get a good idea of how active a scrape is by the amount of leaves/needles in the scrape, resulting from natural falling from the trees. When you hear of a big buck being killed in your hunting area, don't give up. Those unserviced does will be serviced. Another buck will be ready and able to take up where the dead buck left off, and probably using the same travel areas! However, the replacement buck may not be as big as the first.

Rubs (Horning Sign) - Antler rubbing against tree trunks, saplings, and bushes begins in September, when the bucks scratch off the velvet covering the new antlers. Note the velvet coating on the buck's antlers in the photo below.

Antler rubbing continues into October and early November, when they are showing status/dominance. Rubs are visual signs, as well as glandular scent marking, coming from glands in the buck's forehead. This rub carries a specific or signature odor, recognized by other bucks as well as does. The tree types most associated with rubs, in the Southeast, are sweet gum, red cedar, dogwood, oaks, maples, and loblolly pine. The tree size varies from pencil size to over two inches in diameter. Rubbing activity peaks in mid-October, as the hierarchy of dominant bucks is being established. Before the does come into heat or estrus, dominant bucks will playfully fight with lesser bucks. After does start coming into heat, this playful fighting may turn to serious battle. The "rattling" of two bucks fighting can be heard for a considerable distance, and other deer may come to watch the excitement. Since serious fights may impact a buck's social status, they will naturally be interested in the results of such battles. Thus, hunters may use "rattling" as a way to coax deer to the gun.

Yearling bucks only make about half the number of rubs as that of mature bucks. Occasionally, a dominant buck will account for about all of the rubs in a given area. Where you find fresh rubs, you normally can find prior year rubs (See examples in photos below). So, when hunting an unfamiliar area, during early bow season, use prior years rubs to help you determine where the trophy bucks hang out. Follow this line of rubbed trees ("rub line"), away from the feeding areas and toward the thick cover areas, to find his bedding area and a good stand.

- ❖ Whitetail's Defenses - Smell, Hearing, and Sight

  Smell - Smell is the deer's primary defense. Don't ever underestimate the deer's sense of smell. What ever you now think it is, multiply it by two, three, or perhaps ten. The hunter's understanding of the deer's intense sense of smell, primarily, determines how successful the hunter is or will become. A whitetail can smell a hunter for one hundred yards if he is wearing clean clothes, has had a recent bath in no-odor soap, and does all of the other things necessary to reduce human odor. Otherwise, the deer could smell the hunter for three to four hundred yards. This point is VERY IMPORTANT for a hunter to understand.

  Hearing - The deer's second most acute sense is its hearing. Those big ears are for hearing you with, and they do the job very well. Deer hear noises of all sorts all day long – nuts falling, wind blowing, squirrels barking, chipmunks chirpings, limbs and dead trees falling, etc. But, they can pick out the sound of a hunter walking, sneezing, coughing, blowing, talking, whispering, taking a tree stand up a tree, etc. for hundreds of yards, and know that it is a threat. Furthermore, they can normally pinpoint the location of a sound to within a few yards. Obviously, the closer a whitetail is to the sound source, the more precisely they can pinpoint that sound. This is VERY IMPORTANT for a hunter to understand.

The clanging of metal against metal, as a hunter walks through the woods with his portable tree stand on his back, deserves a special note. This sound is so unnatural in the woods; deer are warned that the hunter is coming for hundreds of yards. A deer within hearing range will know what tree this hunter went up and avoid that area. If you are sitting in your tree-stand, an hour after daybreak, and a hunter walks under your tree with his clanging sounds or you are unlucky enough to have them go up a tree a hundred yards away, consider relocating to another area when you come in at mid-day.

Sight - Sight is the deer's least dependable sense, but in the woods, their sight is still much better than yours, when it comes to seeing movement. A deer can see a squirrel shake its tail in anger at a hundred yards. Whitetail can see you glowing if your clothing has been washed in detergents with brighteners. They see what you or I can only see with the assistance of an ultraviolet light. You may be wearing the latest camouflage, and not move, and the deer see you, if your clothing were washed in a detergent with brighteners. They cannot see colors, as you and I; however, they can at least distinguish yellows and blues and can pick out a "blob" of a solid color in the midst of natures multicolor, especially if it moves occasionally. If a deer smells or hears you, it will spook and run. If it sees you it may (only may) need confirmation that you are a threat.

Most hunters, that I've known, underestimate the whitetail's senses – especially their sense of smell! As a result, they make little or no effort to minimize spreading scent or to control their scent trail while at their set-up stand. It is far better to overestimate, than underestimate their senses.

❖ Other Defenses – In addition to their three natural senses, the whitetail has some other attributes that contribute to its elusiveness. They have strong survival instincts. The whitetail has incredible stamina and determination to live. Even after receiving a vitals hit with an appropriate deer hunting rifle slug, a whitetail may travel over a mile before dropping, never to get up again. If it receives a superficial hit, like a leg wound, it has an uncanny ability to recover. One eight point I killed had one front leg missing from the joint down. He had a harem of five does with him. If it gets a body hit, it will find a spot of thick cover and lay down, waiting for the blood to coagulate and plug the holes. Once it has regained some strength, it will likely try to move, under cover of darkness, to familiar/safe home territory. The whitetail normally moves in shadow areas, near thick cover, or through thick cover. When it does move through a cleared field, it will normally pick a spot where the open area necks down to minimize its exposure in open area. They may also use fencerows in this case. A deer can slip through blackberry briers, honeysuckle, a clear-cut with thick treetops and new growth, etc. with amazing ease. Whether in such thick cover or in open woods, they are near invisible when they stand in a "frozen" position. The highly agile whitetail can run for miles at 30 mph and can sprint short distances at over 40 mph. I've watched them clear seven-foot fences and broad jump 30-foot roadways with ease – What a beautiful sight. I once observed a doe, running from a dog in a clear-cut, hit the middle of a logging road with her front hooves, after seeing me; pivot her whole body 180 degrees and bound back into the clear-cut. I don't think she even lost her powerful stride while doing the maneuver.

Chapter Two
When Whitetail Move Most

Another important prerequisite to becoming a proficient whitetail deer hunter is to understand when the whitetail move/travel most and why/where. This understanding will help you know when and where to maximize your hunting efforts. Harvest studies show that as many as ninety percent of whitetails bagged availed themselves to hunters, because the deer were moving and exposing themselves during daylight hours. Whitetail travel for food and sex and to evade danger. Accomplishing these needs ties closely to nature. This chapter concentrates on when whitetail tend to move most; so you, the hunter, can maximize your odds during the limited time you can be in the woods.

Keep in mind that whitetails are basically nocturnal animals (move during the night). This is not news to a seasoned whitetail hunter. The inborn dusk-dawn instinct overrides most (but not all) weather factors. If they do most of their moving at night the hunter still may not see many deer during daylight hours, even if they are moving a lot. The instinct to reproduce (the rut) sometimes overrides the nocturnal and weather factors. Human disturbances, deer population, food supply, sex, etc. may alter this instinctive pattern also. The more human scent/sounds/sightings the whitetails experience, the more nocturnal the deer become. This variable can impact the whitetail's daylight movement more than all the other variables combined. My experience in the woods says that the elusive/evasive old bucks with exceptionally large racks are much more nocturnal than other deer. This, no doubt, is one reason that they lived long enough to develop such an impressive "head dress". My sightings of such bucks, over the years, occurred just after it became too dark to see my sights.

❖ Season Impacts - Seasons exert a major impact on deer behavior. The significant variable is the length of daylight. Daylight length affects the production of the deer's hormone, thyroxin. Also, the longer the days the less time deer have to fill their paunch in darkness, and the hungrier they will become between dawn and dusk. The deer's metabolism slows down gradually as the chill factor drops below fifteen to twenty degrees Fahrenheit; therefore, they don't have to move as much, looking for food. Their body just doesn't require as much food. I guess nature protects the deer in this way, because it is during the cold months that their food supply becomes barren. During the warm months, the deer's metabolism is at maximum and they need more food and must move more to get the food. However, during this time of year, the food supply is abundant, so they may not have to move very far to find food – especially during daylight hours. Excluding the impact of more hunters in the woods, and many other variables, you should see three times more deer in November/early-December than you do in late September (early bow season), due to the rut. In reality a hunter may see fewer deer, during this time period, if hunting pressure is fierce enough. Personally, I see more bucks during bow season and they are less cautious than during gun season. Whitetails will definitely move more during the rut period, but whether they move during night or day depends on hunting pressure for that area. Hunters with limited vacation time may want to use this graph to schedule your deer hunting vacations. Don't use it as gospel. It may vary a bit in your area. The further south that you are, the later rut peaks - Extreme north: November 7, mid-country: November 13, and extreme south: November 18. Even these dates may vary a bit from year to year.

23

Seasonal Whitetail Movement

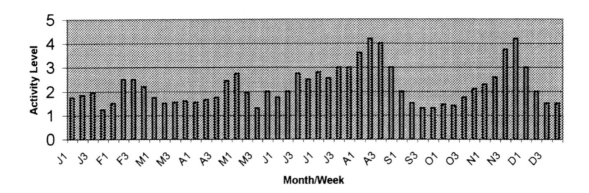

A doe will become many times more active than normal on the night prior to breeding, to assure contact with a buck, and may be seen miles from her normal/small home range. As the doe comes into heat or estrus, the fawns are run off, and you will begin seeing the doe by herself or with a buck. Fawns will be seen traveling alone.

❖ Time of Day Impact - Deer movement peaks the second hour after sunset and the hour just before sunrise. This suggests that we should stay on our stand in the evening until we can't see our sights (a good scope helps) and get to the stand before daylight. More whitetail will frequent open feeding areas in the evening than the early morning. This means maybe we should give higher priority to the evening hunt than the morning hunt. This does not necessarily mean deer are less active in the morning, only that the deer are less observed at this time. They may be as active in the morning, but at that time, hunters are moving to their stand at the same time the deer are active. Whitetail may detect the hunters and move into the thick cover. Studies support the idea that you'll be more successful on the evening hunt. I've seen more deer the last hour of the day and the first two hours of good daylight, during my many years of hunting experience. Personally, I try to give equal priority to morning and evening hunting.

Hunting closer to bedding areas means you'll have a better chance of seeing a deer in the morning, since it's more likely that deer will come by your stand after you are in position. Also in the evening, it allows you the first peek at the deer, as it moves from the bedding area. But, on the other hand, the closer to the bedding area that you hunt, the more trails finger off and fewer deer may be in this area.

- ❖ Weather Impact
  - ➢ Humidity - The lower the humidity, the more deer move. Under normal conditions, the humidity is lower in the afternoon; so whitetail will move more in the afternoon/evening. If humidity were the only variable, deer would move more in mid-afternoon when temperatures are at their highest and humidity is at its lowest. However, the deer's nocturnal (move at night) instinct tends to prevail - at least in most cases. You are more likely to see deer on an evening of low humidity, than on an evening of high humidity. You should see more deer on a warm, clear day than on a cloudy, cool, or stormy day. Don't cancel a hunting trip because of the humidity level. Rather, you may justify still/drive/boat hunting on humid days.
  - ➢ Temperature - During late season and in colder areas, as the temperature rises, deer become more active. However, if the temperature reaches above sixty-five or seventy degrees Fahrenheit, the whitetail's movement begins to decline, and they may look for a cool spot. The whitetail's response to temperature extremes will vary by area. Whitetail adapt to temperature extremes, to some degree. A deer living in Nevada would soon starve if it didn't browse in temperatures above seventy. Similarly, a deer living in up state New York may starve if it refused to browse in temperatures below twenty. High temperatures tend to make deer more nocturnal, since it is cooler at night. Low temperatures tend to make deer less nocturnal, since it is warmer during daylight hours.
  - ➢ Wind - As wind velocity increases, deer activity decreases. You can take this to the bank. The reason is probably due to the deer's senses being rendered less effective. Scents are going every which way, so maybe they can't smell where danger is. Leaves are falling and thrashing, limbs are falling, etc., so maybe they can't hear danger or determine its direction. All the movement in the woods would certainly make it more difficult for them to see danger. During continuously strong winds, you will see only about one third as many deer as when the wind is light, moderate, or occasionally gusty. You may justify using the still hunting method (See Chapter Four and Eight) and walking through cedar thickets, etc. Deer seek shelter in cedar thickets, and other dense evergreens, if the wind chill factor approaches nine degrees Fahrenheit. When the wind chill factor drops below twenty degrees Fahrenheit, deer movement begins to decrease. Dense evergreens moderate the impact of harsh weather. Deer know where the warm places are. In swamps, dense evergreens can have a wind chill twenty degrees Fahrenheit warmer than uplands. Dense evergreens can reduce wind velocity by over half. Deer also seek the sunny sides of hills on bitter cold days. So, if you've got the guts to be out on bitter cold and/or windy days look for these spots. During moderate to strong winds, especially during the late season when the wind chill is severe, you can expect to see little deer

movement, particularly out in open woods. During these times, it is probably best to still hunt or drive hunt areas that afford the deer good protection.

➢ Snow - In snow up to six inches, whitetail can still feed on ground foods by pawing, but deer movement decreases. In deeper snow, they switch to "woody" browsing, and may change their location to do so. Snow, over eighteen inches deep, severely restricts mobility, and they go to cedar, hemlock, laurels, rhododendron, and pine thickets, where the snow is softer, less than half the depth, and they beat out trails in concentrated areas. Deer will return to normal feeding areas as soon as conditions allow. Even in snow depths of twelve inches, deer will take the path of least resistance. They will follow creek-beds, existing beat out trails, etc.

➢ Precipitation - The dryer the season or the day, the better the hunting; however, light rain or snow does not significantly reduce whitetail movement if it's not windy. Heavy rain or snow does reduce movement. Heavy rain or snow motivates whitetail to seek shelter. Look for them in cover that offers umbrella protection. Some people argue that the game may be still moving, but it's the observers/hunters having a problem spotting the deer. On rainy days, whitetails leave their feeding area later than normal, because dawn comes slightly later than it does on a clear day. Dawn also comes quicker. When a night is clear, daylight comes gradually, but on a rainy morning full dark to full light may be only thirty minutes. Late feeding deer may be less cautious, because they are in a hurry to return to the bedding area. If you are hunting from a stand, near the bedding area, on a rainy day, the deer may be less wary when they come by the hunter's set-up position. You may see them in better light, because they are traveling later, since full dark to daylight comes quicker.

➢ Barometric pressure - Prior to 1978, most game biologists had not correlated barometric pressure to deer activity. By 1980 they seemed to agree that deer movement increased with a falling barometer. Generally, high-pressure means clear and stable weather and low-pressure means poor and unstable weather. Whitetails often move extremely well, during a falling pressure, before the bad weather moves in. The falling barometric pressure apparently tells deer that bad weather is coming. They will sometimes move better than usual during a rising barometer following bad weather, because their stomachs are probably near empty. Deer will move more if the barometric pressure is high and steady (nice weather) than if it is low and steady (bad weather). I know that the barometric pressure drops as a major fall storm moves into an area, and I am positive that deer sometimes move like crazy in this situation. This increased movement is more apparent before some fronts move through than others; therefore, I've concluded that the rate that the barometric pressure falls, and/or the amount of wind accompanying the weather change also has a significant bearing. This infrequent combination of weather factors possibly has the most significant positive impact on deer movement than any other weather situation, and would definitely merit remaining at your stand all day long (or, until it starts raining hard). This is contrary to some articles that I've read. Once, a three-day front was moving into my hunting area, while the wind was calm, and I could have killed three bucks in eighteen hours. Furthermore, on my way out that evening and back the next morning, before the front entered my area, I saw deer herd after deer herd. I told my buddy, "This situation occurs less than one day per month. There has got to be a major front moving in", and there was. Hunt hard the last twelve to eighteen hours prior to a major front moving in (falling pressure), using the stand method. Once the front moves in, deer movement all but stops, and you may be better off still-hunting or drive hunting. Ends of long bad storms should be good hunting also. The whitetails' stomachs are empty, and they're looking for food. Should we whitetail hunters carry a barometer in our vehicle? Definitely yes!

➢ Cloud cover - You may see one third more deer on a clear day than a cloudy or overcast day. However, maybe this statistic is partly due to the observers having better visibility on clear days?

❖ Moon Impact - Spot-lighters say they don't see many whitetails in the fields when the moon is shining bright. Deer feel more secure in fields on dark nights; so, they tend to browse more in wooded areas on moonlit nights. This means whitetail will not tend to move toward fields in the late evening or away from fields in the morning as much when the moon is bright. Whitetails definitely move more during daylight hours on days following a dark night. Some hunters say that deer tend to get up with the moon and rest when it is gone (regardless if the moon is up during the day or night). They say that whitetails tend to feed into the day after the moon has risen or is about to rise. Hunting pressure would obviously change this daylight-feeding tendency. They concluded: new moon - excellent hunting, quarter moon - good hunting, half moon - fair hunting, and full moon - poor hunting. I remember an early bow season hunt, when the moon was rising bright/full near dusk and setting near daylight. On an evening hunt, I shot at (and missed) a nice buck at 4:00 PM (over two and one half hours before dark), and I saw him again the next morning, as I was walking from my stand, at 10:00 AM (over three and one half hours after good daylight). I think that it's safe to conclude that you should stand hunt closer to bedding areas during the full moons, and you should consider staying on your stand longer in the morning during full moon. Now, if the moon only shined brightly for the first half of the night, it may not significantly impact the morning hunt. If the moon only shined brightly the last half of the night, it may not significantly impact the evening hunt. Personally, I prefer hunting during the new moon.

❖ Summary of When Deer Move Most (Pardon my duplication, but this is VERY IMPORTANT.)
  ➢ Seasonal - Deer move most in August to early September and late October to early December. A doe will become many times more active than normal, on the night prior to breeding, to assure contact with a buck.
  ➢ Time of day - Give higher priority (or at least equal) to the evening hunt than the morning hunt.
  ➢ Humidity - The lower the humidity, the more deer move.
  ➢ Temperature - Deer movement begins to decline if the temperature drops below twenty degrees Fahrenheit or if it climbs above sixty-five or seventy degrees Fahrenheit.
  ➢ Wind and air chill - During continuously strong winds, you will see only about one third as many deer as when the wind is light, moderate, or occasionally gusty.
  ➢ Precipitation - During a heavy rain or snow deer movement all but stops. If you are hunting from a stand near the bedding area on a rainy day, the deer may be less wary. You may see them in better light, because they are traveling later, and because full dark to daylight comes quicker.
  ➢ Barometric pressure - Hunt hard the last twelve to eighteen hours prior to a major front moving in, when the barometric pressure is dropping rapidly.
  ➢ Cloud cover - You may see one third more deer on a clear day than a cloudy or overcast day.
  ➢ Moon impact - Whitetails definitely move more during daylight hours on days following a dark night. You should stand hunt closer to bedding areas, during the full moons, and may consider staying on your stand longer in the morning, during full moons.

Chapter Three
Selecting an Area to Hunt

After learning the whitetail hunting skills and how to apply them, selecting the best general areas to hunt probably impacts the hunters' success most of all the other variables. Whitetail population and terrain/vegetation are probably the most important variables to consider when selecting an area to hunt. Whitetail kill statistics, by county, is the simplest way to find good whitetail populations. Driving, walking, studying topographic maps, and talking to other hunters can help the hunter find acceptable terrain/vegetation areas, within the counties having a good whitetail population.

❖ State/County/Area to Hunt - Becoming a proficient whitetail hunter requires that you do your homework. Collect whitetail kill statistics to help you determine the best state and counties to hunt. The Wildlife Resource Agencies of the state(s), convenient for you to hunt, have good data these days, and will be glad to share it with you. This data should be available on their Internet web pages or you may call them at the phone numbers listed in the Appendix. Following are estimated deer populations and harvest numbers, taken from the Appendix, for those states having impressive whitetail populations:

	Latest Popul. (000)	Latest Harv. (000)	Highest Harvest Co./Areas	% Permit Success	Record Scores
AL	1750.0	400.0		60.2	
AR	1000.0	194.7	Union		T79&AT184
GA	1300.0	375.0			
IL	700.0	135.3	Pike/Adams	35.0	T200 2/8 B&C
IN	500.0	98.7	Steuben/Swizerland		T195 1/8&AT248 4/8
KY	750.0	157.0	Lawrence/Ohio	48.0	T189&AT243 3/8 290#
LA	1000.0	267.5	Areas 1 & 2	50.0	T184 6/8&AT281 6/8
MI	1900.0	544.9	South MI	58.0	T186.1& AT238.2
MN	960.0	143.3		29.0	
MS	1500.0	300.0	Along MS River		T182.8 7/8&AT255 6/8
MO	950.0	245.8	Units 3 & 7	35.0	205.00
NY	1000.0	294.6	Allegheny/Cattaraugus		
NC	900.0	212.5	North Hampton	49.0	181.88
OH	500.0	149.7	Muskingum's/Athens	33.3	
PA	1500.0	377.5	Bradford/Washington		T189&AT213 6/9
SC	1000.0	300.0	Williamsburg/Orangeb.	76.0	T176BC&AT208 5/8BC
TN	990.0	155.7	Henry/Humphrey	55.3	
TX	3500.0	399.9	Gillespie/Llano	54.0	T196 4/8AT286
VA	900.0	186.5	Loudon/Bedford	60.2	T188 6/8&AT257 4/8
WI	1250.0	362.6	Marathon	57.0	T206 1/8&AT245
WV	900.0	195.3	Lewis/Mason	25.0	T182 3/8AT237 5/8

See the Appendix for other states.

Collect maps of Wildlife Management Areas that you may be interested in hunting. Buy a good topographic map book of the states that you may be interested in hunting. I use one by DeLorme, P.O. Box 298, Yarmouth, Maine 04096, (207) 846-7000, http://www.delorme.com. Request hunting and trapping guide handbooks for states that you intend to hunt. They will give you the laws of the state, Wildlife Management Areas and their hunt dates, etc. Get familiar with the license, permits, big game stamps, etc. required. Some states offer a general sportsman's license that covers all fees.

If deer size is important to you, some areas have much larger deer than others. Body size of adult deer can range from under one hundred pounds to over two hundred pounds. Ten-point rack widths can vary from ten inches to twenty-five plus inches, and their base diameter can vary from roughly one-half inch to two inches. See Chapter Nine, Hunting Trophy Bucks. Travel time to potential hunting areas has historically dictated the areas that I hunt. If you enjoy camping, this may not be an important issue. Camping near a hunting area could make your hunting trip a family affair. Some hunters prefer staying in a hotel, near their hunting area, while on a hunting trip. I've done them all and each has advantages. Season and/or bag limit laws will vary from state to state, and even within a given state, so this too may enter into your decision analysis.

Once you've determined which counties have good whitetail populations, try to determine the best areas within these counties. Just because a certain county has a good population, does not mean that all areas within that county have a good population. Travel to specific potential areas, especially if you're considering joining a hunting club in that area. A near ideal hunting area has bedding areas (thick cover) and pastures/meadows/fields with a good stretch of somewhat open woods in-between. Hopefully, you could set up toward the bedding area, without deer detecting your presence, as they move from the fields, for the morning hunt. An example of a poor hunting area (even if the population is good) is as follows: You have an opportunity to lease ninety acres. All of the property is pasture except ten acres of open hardwoods in one corner. First, you would run the deer out of your leased property, as you drove in for the morning hunt. Second, ten acres of cover, even good cover, is not enough area to hunt. Third, where is bedding (thick cover)? If it is a mile off, morning deer would be long gone when you got to your stand (assuming you didn't run your deer out as you drove/walked in). Evening deer may not get to your stand until after you're driving home, and mid-day snackers probably are not coming out into the pasture, in broad daylight.

The distance you have to walk to your stand may be an important variable to you. Neighborhood dogs running in an area may be a problem. Livestock having access to an area does not seem to pose a problem, except maybe separating deer sign from livestock sign (goats especially).

❖ Public vs. Private Land - I prefer hunting where there are few or no other hunters. In this case deer are following their normal routines and the sign that you read is more meaningful. This is why I prefer hunting private lands. If there are too many hunters in an area, you use the luck method of hunting, regardless of how good a hunter you are. I don't get much pleasure out of luck hunting (See Chapter Four under "Luck Hunting").

➢ Public - Wildlife Management Areas provides thousands of acres on which to hunt. We hunters pay for its management with our hunting license fees, stamp fees, permit fees, taxes, etc. They also get revenue from allowing timber to be harvested, mineral rights, etc. All hunters share public properties. This means that you may scout and find the perfect stand, and on the morning of the hunt you may have trouble finding a place to park, much less a somewhat private place to hunt. This means you may think you have an all around perfect place to hunt, and other hunters walk under your tree with clanging tree stands, sit down under your tree, etc. It means that the deer are all of a sudden bombarded with human scent/noise/sightings. Deer may not continue following their normal trails or using their normal feeding or bedding areas; therefore, the sign that you read may not be meaningful for picking a good stand. Following are a few points that may improve your whitetail hunting success when you are hunting a Wildlife Management Area (WMA) or other areas where hunter competition is fierce.

Locate several alternative stands prior to the hunt if you can. Ignore the deer sign to some degree. Rather, ask yourself where the deer are going, when bombarded with all of us hunters? Especially on opening gun season day, hunt on escape routes deer may travel, when they are bombarded with human scent/noise/sightings: saddles, low places in bluffs, ends of long slews, swamps having some dry spots, etc. Look for trails entering such areas, for a setup stand. These trails may be barely visible before significant hunting pressure is sensed by the elusive whitetails. You may be better off anticipating where the fewest hunters will be, rather than where the most deer are. If you can read the heavy trails, especially road sign, most other hunters can also. Don't make the mistake of looking at the map, finding the most remote road, and driving to the very end. So many times I've done this, only to find that many other hunters piled up at the end of these remote roads also. You're probably better off to scout half way down such roads and find a spot, even if it doesn't have quite as heavy sign. Consider hunting difficult to get to places. Most hunters aren't going to walk up very steep terrain, around swampy slews, through briers and brambles, a mile or so deep where even an ATV can't get to, etc. to find a deer. Look for areas that, at first glance, seem so thick that it's impossible to hunt. Now, look beyond the thick growth. It may open up into beautiful hardwoods. Scouting the transition, between the thick growth and the hardwoods, may result in potentially good hunting. If your "honey-hole" is over run with other hunters on the first weekend, be patient. Most hunters "fizzle-out" after a couple of weeks into the season and you may find that you have it to yourself then. If your work schedule allows, hunt WMA's during weekdays, when many other hunters must punch a time clock. This ploy works! Stay in the woods longer than the other hunters. Go to your stand early and leave late. There is a good chance other hunters will run a deer to you, as they walk in or out. When the other hunters become restless at their stands and start walking, they will dislodge deer. Consider hunting on the ground. By hunting on the ground, you can easily reposition if other hunters surround you, and you do not have to worry about someone stealing an expensive tree stand. If you use a portable tree stand, make sure to secure it to the tree when you leave it unattended, using a chain or cable and lock. I've lost a couple that I failed to secure. If you have to hunt where there are going to be several other hunters, use their scent to your advantage. Either locate upwind far enough that the hunter next to you will not impact your hunt or go far enough downwind that their scent will cause deer to dodge them and come by you. Ignore the more popular WMA's. Scout small WMA's or WMA's that are cut-up into many small, separated, and perhaps inconvenient to get to places. I've found a couple of these and have found little competition on them after opening day.

➢ Private property

Corporate property - Paper, timber, and land companies sometimes lease big tracts to hunting clubs, but sometimes they allow individual permits to be purchased for rather small fees. A big part of this land will probably be pines. Although deer seem to thrive in pine, I've never been crazy about hunting in pines, because it is difficult for me to read sign in pines and hard to track a wounded deer in them.

Hunting clubs - When anywhere from two to hundreds of hunters pay dues to hunt on property, a hunting club exists. The club may post the property with "No Hunting" signs or may hire it done. Fees for hunting clubs can vary from under a hundred dollars per year to hundreds, depending on the number of club members, number of acres leased, cost per acre per year, etc. The higher the number of huntable leased acres per club member (and their guests, family, etc.) the more private your hunting and the less the deer will spook, you'll be bothered with other hunters, etc. In some cases you may have less privacy than using public property. Depending on this property's location, its ability to be secured, etc., spotlighting, road hunters, and dog hunters may impact your success. Before forking over money for fees, you should personally scout the area and know what you are buying. The club should be willing to let you hunt a day or two before "buying in".

Relatives and friends - If you have friends or relatives who own a hundred acres or so in an area with a good deer population, and they are willing to let you hunt on it, consider yourself a lucky hunter. Once you get permission, don't ruin it by shooting cows, leaving gates open, riding down fences, or leaving drink cans and other trash on their property – even deep in the woods. I'm a landowner and all this really irritates me.

Arrangements with farmers - When I've found an area with an exceptional deer population, I've actually gone door-to-door asking permission to hunt. If you tell the farmer that you only want permission to archery hunt and/or only you will be hunting, it helps. Once they see that you respect their property and they get to know you, they may allow a second person and/or other type hunting. You may be entertained listening to stories about what hunters have done to these good folk in the past. When trying to get permission to hunt, be honest and let them know how you hunt and where you want to hunt on the property. People are normally skeptical of strangers. You may offer to help them if they are performing some farm task. Once, when an old lady gave me permission to hunt, I noticed her porch was caving in. I built her a new treated pine porch and am still welcome to hunt there, many years later. Again, once you get permission, don't ruin it by disrespecting their property. Also, get their address and send them a thank you note when you get back home. Send them a Christmas card and/or bring them a gift from time to time. I raise a garden, and there are times that I have much more garden produce than I can use. Guess who I prefer taking my surplus produce to. Right, the good people letting me hunt on their property, that can not raise a garden.

Residential or industrial areas for archery season - Sometimes you find a subdivision with many vacant lots, a golf course zigzagging through a wooded setting, a city park or reservoir, a large shrub-nursery with some timber nearby, an industrial site with several wooded acres in the rear, etc. that may be home for a respectable herd of whitetail. Gun hunting in such areas would seldom be legal, but bow hunting may be acceptable. Sometimes residents become irritated by the whitetails eating their expensive shrubs, making trails through their yard, or damaging the well-manicured golf course "greens". I've seen some whopper bucks in such settings. It makes me want to give "hole in one" a whole new meaning. These whitetails should be easier to hunt, since they are accustomed to smelling/hearing/seeing humans, but don't under estimate their elusiveness or evasiveness. I've spent a bit of time hunting a couple of them and I haven't put a residential/industrial whitetail on the wall yet, but I will!

Buy your own land - If you can afford it, this can be a wonderful alternative. The advantage here is that you have more control over the hunting area. You can choose who hunts your land to some degree. Whitetail sign, that you read, will be more meaningful, because the whitetail's normal routine will not be affected by human activity. Securing the property from spot lighting, road hunters, and dog hunters is more controllable. Sometimes you can buy a tract of land that backs up to other property, or has places nearby that you can hunt, giving you even more hunting area. This alternative allows the hunter to build a small cabin or set a camper on it; thus, eliminating hotel bills and/or long drives to and from the hunting area.

Hunting Cabin Layout

3/5/00

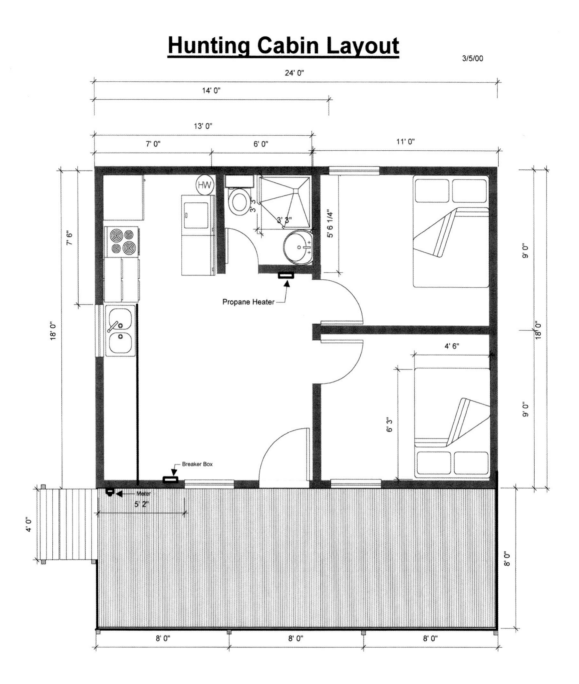

If you're really a dedicated whitetail hunter, consider buying property in prime whitetail country and building your retirement home there. Having good hunting in your "back door" is a real luxury.

Chapter Four
Overview of Methods to Harvest Whitetail

The objective of this chapter is to explain why I recommend, "stand hunting" as the primary hunting method. To accomplish this objective, I will briefly outline all methods to hunt the whitetail - legal and illegal. Then I will explain why resorting to illegal methods is unnecessary to become a highly successful whitetail hunter. Following are eight methods of harvesting whitetail deer:

❖ Stand hunting - This method is where you find a spot in an area with a reasonably good deer population, and where the sign, terrain, etc. tell you the deer are traveling, feeding, or bedding, and sit and wait for the deer. If the hunter can read sign to determine where the deer are, the hunter can wait in ambush at a good vantage point until the target of his choice comes by. This book provides in depth instructions on how to master this method to harvest the whitetail. This method requires considerable skill and is highly rewarding when you succeed. You may not kill as many deer as you would spotlighting, but you may kill more trophies, and you will not have to worry about reading of your arrest in the newspaper. Statistically, this method is more effective than the other legal hunting methods. This method is taught is Chapters Five through Seven. To maximize your effectiveness/proficiency, as a whitetail hunter, choose "stand hunting" as your primary hunting method. Use still, driving, and boat hunting methods in the middle of the day, all day on those days conditions render stand hunting less effective, or any other time whitetail movement declines.

❖ Still hunting - This method is where the hunter moves slowly and quietly through the woods, looking as deep into the woods ahead as he can train his eye to look. This method requires significant skill. You need to know how/where to walk, making minimum noise, while being as invisible to the whitetail as possible. This is a legal hunting method and is a nice fill-in between the morning and evening hunts. During certain weather conditions, it is more productive than stand hunting. This method is taught in Chapter Eight.

❖ Drive hunting - This method is where one or more hunter walk through or by a potential bedding and/or feeding area and, hopefully, causes a deer or two to move toward the buddy hunter or hunters and it requires significant skill. This method is legal and too is a nice fill-in between the morning and evening hunts. During certain weather conditions, it too is more productive than stand hunting. This method is taught in Chapter Eight.

❖ Boat hunting - Using a boat to get to otherwise isolated areas opens up a world of opportunity. Also, cruising the shorelines looking for bedded or browsing whitetail is a novel approach to still hunting. This method is taught in Chapter Eight.

❖ Dogging - When dogs run a deer, the deer will normally take the same escape route, and/or may run in a circle, so you place someone at road crossings, etc. to shoot the deer as it comes through. Some hunters use tracking collars on the dogs so they can tell exactly where the deer is at all times the chase is on. This method requires the hunter to be a good shot. Many shots are long range, and the deer is normally running at top speed. This method is quite effective but is illegal in most areas. You can't get too fond of your dogs if you use this method. Some hunters become very irritated when they're up a tree with a bow in bow season and dogs run under their tree and rifles are firing around them. Some zealous game wardens may shoot these dogs also. Most hunters, using this method that I know, prefer hunting outside of legal gun seasons to avoid losing dogs. This method is not taught within this book.

❖ Luck hunting - This method is perhaps the simplest hunting method of all. Simply drive out of town and stop at some woods, walk into the woods and sit down. You don't dare do any scouting or some of the luck factor may be removed. Or, you pick a place that you know there

36

will be many other hunters and someone is bound to run a deer toward you. Or, pick a stand overlooking a large open area. There should be something run through such a large area. This method requires absolutely no skill. This method is where the hunter has no plan, or a poor plan based on erroneous information, knows nothing about whitetail habits or habitat, does no preparation, has all the wrong equipment, and just simply does everything wrong. The only good thing that I can say about this method is that it is legal. This method is used by a significant percent of whitetail hunters and once in a while they too kill a deer. This method is not taught or recommended within this book.

❖ Road hunting - This method is simple. All you have to do is drive the roads and logging roads until you spot a deer, aim and shoot. It does work best if you train your eye to pick up a deer deep in the woods or the back corner of a pasture field. You probably ought to learn where the houses are too. You'd hate to shoot one at the edge of someone's yard, or, worse yet, shoot through his or her house. This method requires the hunter to be a good shot. Many shots may be long range. This method is very effective and is illegal anywhere in the United States. You've got to be careful not to shoot the game warden's fake deer. That would get you in big trouble. Some state authorities call these fake deer "Timex", because they take a shooting and keep on ticking. This method is not taught or recommended within this book.

❖ Spotlighting - This method too is simple and illegal anywhere in the United States. All you have to do is shine a high-powered light around the perimeter of a field at night until your light picks up the deer's eyes, then aim and shoot. This method is so effective that, if all hunters used it, there would soon be no whitetail deer left to hunt. I'm sure this is why it is an illegal method. If the deer doesn't drop immediately, after you shoot, don't worry about looking for it, because you may get caught. Besides, spotlighters say it's easier to just go to the next field and shoot another. This is not very sporting and when you brag about your kills, make sure you don't tell what method you used. Also, you better be careful that no one sees the eyes of your kills. The pupil will be dilated, which is a dead give away that it was a night kill. That could be embarrassing, or could get you put in jail. This method is not taught or recommended within this book. Road hunting and spotlighting is no more a sport than shooting a farmer's cow, while it is standing in the middle of a pasture field. What sense of accomplishment and gratification could a person possibly enjoy from using these lazy methods to harvest a whitetail?

Discussion - Why are there so many spot-lighters, road hunters, etc.? Could it be that many of those people have not had an opportunity to learn how to become a skillful hunter, using ethical/legal methods? Do they resort to methods that are easier to master after becoming frustrated by not killing deer while attempting to use legal methods? At a manufacturing plant, where I worked about fifteen years ago, I met Rick, who showed me a photo of three deer in the back of his pickup. I thought, "I've found a mentor – someone to answer all of my questions". Wrong - The area foreman told me that Rick spotlighted those deer. He normally took his twelve year old daughter spotlighting; thus, appearing less suspicious to a game warden. Rick later told me that he hunted for years, using legal hunting methods, and never killed a single deer. So he started spotlighting and started killing truckloads. But what Rick didn't know was that learning to be a skillful hunter, and killing one or two deer per season using ethical/legal methods, probably would have given him much more reward and satisfaction than all of those spotlighted kills. If you know someone like Rick, introduce him or her to this book. This book can make becoming a skillful and legal whitetail hunter very simple and a lot more rewarding than using illegal methods.

Those kills that I've made using the stand method, I am most proud of. This method, to me, requires the most skill and is the most rewarding of all. There's something about matching wits with the instincts of the elusive/evasive whitetail and winning. Studying this book will teach you all you need to know to become a highly skilled and ethical whitetail hunter. Then you'll have to apply what you've learned, find a good area to hunt, and be persistent in your pursuit of the whitetail. Think of this book as a reference book and keep it handy for future reference. This book doesn't have long entertaining stories. Rather, it was written to teach anyone wanting to learn to hunt the whitetail how to do so and to teach deer hunters how to become better deer hunters.

Chapter Five
Stand Hunting - Picking Stand Location

Once you've selected the area with a good deer population, that you want to hunt, it's time to develop your strategy, based on accurate intelligence. To develop a good strategy you must determine the deer's travel pattern and pick the near perfect stand. This means you must determine where they are eating, where they are bedding, and how they are moving between the food source and bedding. If it's after mid October, where are the scrapes? In other words, scout the area. Remember the analogy in Chapter One comparing the Allies liberating Kuwait in operation Desert Storm to whitetail hunting? This chapter will teach you how to gather accurate intelligence on your adversary, how to develop a strategy based on this intelligence and, therefore, how to win your battle with the whitetail.

❖ Travel Pattern - The majority of whitetails are killed while traveling to primary feeding in the evening, away from primary feeding in the morning, and when they feed briefly in secondary feeding areas, around their bedding areas, sometime during the day. Therefore, the whitetail hunter must analyze the hunting area, and determine where primary feeding is located, and where bedding areas are located. The hunter must determine what routes they are taking, between bedding and primary feeding, and where they may come out of their bedding area for a midday snack. Terrain, available cover, and obstacles (fences, gullies, lakes, creeks, swamps, etc.) will tell you where to look for these routes.

Primary feeding areas - This is a major food source that motivates deer to travel miles, if necessary, to put ten to twenty pounds of food in their paunch. Primary feeding areas are normally in little or no cover areas, requiring the whitetail to feed in total darkness. This may be a farmer's hay field, soybeans, etc., lush valley meadow, a Wildlife Management Area's food plot, or some other favorite and bountiful food source. On clear nights, when the moon shines bright all night long, whitetail may not use primary feeding areas. Rather, they may browse in secondary feeding areas all night. Primary feeding spots for the whitetail will probably change in late season, after the first few hard freezes kill most of the grass/hay and they dry up. Now the primary feeding areas may become some portion of these grass fields, that were protected from the freezes, and remained green; or, it may become a winter wheat cover crop further away, large honeysuckle patches, cane breaks, large acorns in open woods, etc.

Secondary feeding areas - Deer use these for midday browsing and also for browsing to and from primary feeding areas. When the moon shines bright all night long, the whitetails may use secondary feeding areas as primary feeding areas. Before whitetails sense hunting pressure, secondary feeding areas will be about any area offering food and some degree of cover. After hunting pressure increases, the whitetail's secondary feeding areas shrink. They limit their midday browsing to within their thick cover bedding area, and, maybe, in the area immediately surrounding the bedding area.

Bedding area - In early season, before deciduous trees lose their leaves and before whitetail start smelling/hearing/sighting humans, this may be open woods with fair under-brush or it may be the areas having thick cover. By thick cover, I mean clear-cuts, young cedar thickets, hemlock groves, matted honeysuckle thickets, laurel and rhododendron thickets, steep bluffs, a high place in the middle of a swamp, or anywhere else that is virtually impossible for a human to even crawl through. After the deciduous trees lose their leaves, and whitetail start smelling/hearing/sighting humans, bedding will normally be thick cover. It will definitely be a dry spot. Whitetails will wade water up to their belly or swim a lake or river, but the whitetail insists on a well-drained spot to lie down for a nap.

When starting to hunt a new area, it is VERY IMPORTANT to learn the general travel pattern of the deer as quickly as possible. Travel patterns change as food supplies and cover change; so, rethink travel patterns as seasons change, land is cleared or cut, etc. Consider that whitetail leave the bedding area toward (or after) dark and travel toward their primary feeding area (say, a farmer's winter wheat cover crop) munching on acorns, etc. along the way. They travel slowly and normally stay in thick cover, especially if they smell/hear/see humans in their area. During this time shooting light is lessening. Thus, stands near bedding areas are more productive than stands near primary feeding areas, especially after deciduous trees drop their leaves (whitetail lose their cover) and become spooked from human activity. This is contrary to a lot of articles that I've read. In the evening it is more likely that deer will come under your tree, headed to feed, before it gets full dark, if you hunt near thick cover (bedding areas). Deer leave the feeding areas at a time to allow them to be nearing their beds at daylight. During this time shooting light improves. In the morning, it is more likely that deer will come by your tree just after daylight, if you hunt near bedding areas. Deer start fanning out to various bedding spots as close as a few hundred yards from a primary feeding area. They may continue branching off for miles. Anywhere you hunt, you may be hunting near some deer's bed, especially early in the season before the leaves fall and the deer lose this

40

cover. Also, if you hunt too close to a primary feeding area, you probably will run them out as you walk to your stand in the morning, unless you are lucky enough to find an accessible back way in. Heavily traveled trails will often be found near the deer's primary feeding area. So, don't be too quick to pick a deep and muddy trail for your stand. Another reason to select a stand near bedding areas is that in addition to the sometimes-long trips to their primary feeding areas, they like to browse in or adjacent to their bedding area for midday snacks. The hunter that picks a stand over deep and muddy trails, at the primary feeding area, will miss most of the midday snackers. A final reason to select a stand near bedding areas is that a wise old buck may have four or more entrances/exits to/from bedding. Some of these trails merge together near bedding; therefore, the closer to bedding (where there are fewer or possibly even just one trail) that you hunt, the greater the odds you have of intercepting the buck.

Realize though, if you hunt too close to the buck's bedding area you will spook him into relocating. But, if you are positive he's coming to this spot, it may be worth the risk. Normally, the hunter can hunt close to the bedroom and not risk spooking the buck into relocating. But, sometimes the terrain, air currents, etc. may make this a poor choice. So, if you've only got a day or two to hunt, and you have four or five trails leading to the bedroom, go straight to his bedroom. I got a trophy last year during archery season by hunting his bed. I found a huge bed on the peak of a very thick mountaintop. Next morning I was there at daylight. At one and one-half hour after daylight, I saw him come in like a ghost. He came straight to his spot and lay down - no walking around. He was forty yards from me and behind two trees. I grunt called twice but he ignored me. At twelve noon the wind started switching and he got a faint scent of me. He got up and moved toward me, under the large leafed undergrowth to twenty feet, looking up at me all the way. I made a between the shoulder blade shot. This was one of the most exciting mornings that I've spent in the woods. Obviously, hunting a buck's bedroom would only work as a morning stand.

Whitetails normally move uphill toward bedding in the morning and downhill toward primary feeding areas in the evening, but there are lots of exceptions to this. For example, in early bow season they may be bedding near creeks and swamps where it is cool. During bitter cold they may seek low areas, where they find dense evergreens to moderate the impact of harsh weather. Also, primary feeding, or the route to and/or from primary feeding, may be higher than, say, a clear-cut or swamp they are bedding in.

It behooves the hunter to drive and walk until he knows the feeding and bedding areas. You should be familiar with what is in a five-mile radius of your hunting spot. Four-wheelers (ATV's) are great for finding general, over-all travel patterns, but don't over-use them. They do not work for finding detail sign. Get off the ATV and walk. I remember watching two hunters on new four-wheel drive ATV's "scouting" an area that I took several nice bucks from. They drove all through it and I never saw them again. They just didn't see, from their ATV's, what I saw walking.

Try to determine if deer are simply traveling back and forth, between bedding and feeding, or using a circle. Do not assume that deer will travel a straight line between feeding and bedding. Sometimes deer take a very long way around, if required to stay in good cover, especially during daylight hours. If they can be using a circle, are they moving clockwise or counter-clockwise? You need to know this to determine where to morning hunt and where to evening hunt. Hoof print direction may tell you this, but sometimes spending time at your stand is the only way to accurately make this decision. If they are using a back and forth movement, how many alternative routes could they take? Most of the time it ends up being a crapshoot, but the more you learn about their travel routine, the better your odds of picking your stand location where you'll see deer. Are there any spots between feeding and bedding that the cover is more narrow, or otherwise force the deer to funnel through a narrow area?

You may consider using infrared scouting camera(s) if you have limited hunting time. Mount one to a tree near a trail or scrape, which you plan to hunt, and you'll get a picture with date and time when an animal of significant size passes. Now you know how big the buck is and when he is coming through. They are rather expensive, may be a theft problem in some hunting areas, and setting it up and retrieving the film may spread scent and spook some deer.

❖ Funneling Them to You - Learning to use funnels is essential to the bow/crossbow hunter, who needs to get the whitetail within thirty yards for an effective shot. Mastering this ploy will also improve the gun hunter's success. This is a VERY IMPORTANT concept necessary to become a highly skilled whitetail hunter.
  ➤ Hunt near scrapes - Most good hunters agrees that this is the best place to kill a trophy. The buck will probably approach from the safest (thickest/into-the-wind) direction but not necessarily. The buck may come in downwind, over a hundred yards away, and rely on his smell to determine if a doe in heat has been there. If you place some Tink's #69 Doe-In-Rut doe urine (or equivalent) in the scrape you are watching, and a few drops on all four sides of your stand, but in view from your stand, you will improve the chances of seeing the buck. The idea is that the deer smell the lure scent trail, before moving into your scent trail, and divert toward the lure scent location; thus, missing your scent trail. Stay on your stand all day long. Your probability of success is high. This is one case that it would probably pay to spend more than one day on the same stand.

  The conditions of scrapes/rubs change. Key ones disappear and new ones appear due to (1) changes in food supply and/or changes in bedding locations, (2) hunting pressure, (3) he's elsewhere chasing a doe in heat, (4) peak rut is passing or (5) someone else killed your buck. Evaluate trails around scrapes. Try to determine where the buck is bedding, and his likely approach to/from his bed. Find about three locations you could set up your stand. This gives you flexibility for varying wind directions, throwing him off guard by changing stand locations, or competing with other hunters for a productive stand. Approach a scrape no closer than necessary to minimize spreading scent. Move in and out quickly/quietly, when checking scrapes, and don't move through heavy cover where the buck may be bedding.

  Many hunters go crazy over what they perceive as the peak rut weeks, and I guess this is fine if you have only one vacation week to hunt (unless, many other hunters in your hunting area had the same reasoning). Trophy bucks are a bit more careless during the peak than they are during the early and late rut weeks, assuming equal hunting pressure. If you observe the size of fawns when you hunt, it is obvious that their size/spots vary considerably. It is obvious that they were born over a one to two month period of time. Therefore, they must have been conceived over a similar time period. All does do not come into heat the same day, or week, or probably not the same month, and those does that did not "catch" the first time they came into heat will come into heat again later. Once the first scrapes appear and the first doe comes into heat a week or two later, bucks will begin to become more active, start responding to the hunter's rut calls, etc. This whole rut period is a fine time to hunt the whitetail, and hunting the scrapes, during this period, is a fine way to put a trophy on the wall! Pick your stand as far downwind of the scrape area as decent visibility and your shooting device allows. If the big buck decides to check his scrapes by circling down wind of the scrapes, you'll have higher odds of seeing the buck and the buck will have lower odds of smelling you, the hunter. The gun hunter should position to see as much of the scrape area as possible; the bow hunters must position themselves within bow range of the scrape, or on one of the bucks' likely approaches to the scrape(s). If you can not find a suitable stand location near a scrape, try creating a scent trail from the scrape to your stand by spraying Tink's #69 Doe-In-Rut doe urine (or equivalent) on bushes/ground between the scrape and your stand. Remember, if a buck checks a scrape and smells a hot doe, he will likely start tracking the hot doe. An alternative to this ploy may be creating an additional scrape, close to existing scrapes, near your preferred stand set-up location. Afternoon hunting is normally best for hunting over scrapes. Some say bucks visit scrapes long after the last doe is serviced.

➢ Favorite foods (See Chapter One under "Food") - It's not uncommon for a deer to come to these spots for a mid-day snack, especially if their bedding area is nearby. In early bow season, when acorns just begin to fall, look for oaks with near full sun. Acorns may drop here first. Look for oaks in the middle of clear-cuts. In dry seasons look at oaks in low places. Acorns may drop here earlier or may be the only trees bearing that year. During seasons when late frosts/freezes killed oak blooms, look at the oaks on the hillsides protecting the oaks. Small acorns or beechnuts, in an area where there're few or none on the ground for a mile or so around, is probably a good stand, especially if they are near or in the middle of thick growth. Look for secluded offsets of a pasture field still green after freezes have killed most grass. Also, a farmer's winter wheat cover crop, surrounded with good cover, may work. Deer will seek out green grass if it is available. Well-fertilized grass will stay green much longer than poorly or average fertilized grass. Invest in a few bags of 19-19-19 fertilize and spread it in these secluded corners where you can get a shot from your stand. During late gun season, even bucks can't resist the temptation to feed on scarce green grass.

➢ Gullies - Deer take the path of least resistance, unless they are spooked. Show me a long deep gully, and I'll show you a dandy trail at either the top end, bottom end, or somewhere in between that it is shallow.

➢ Benches (shelves) on steep slopes - This is a path of easier walking and likely will have a good trail.

➢ Ends of long slews - If you're hunting around a lake, check out the long slews. Slews funnel deer at their apex.

➢ Narrow spots in large wooded areas - I especially love these. They are so predictable, especially if they are in or near thick cover. When good cover necks down at a point, say between two big fields, there will be more than one good trail coming close together. If there aren't good trails here, the deer population is probably poor.

➢ Wide thick fencerows, with perhaps a few giant oaks along the way, may funnel deer. Oaks in fencerows get maximum sun, and may start dropping acorns before oaks in heavily wooded areas. Such fencerows may offer adequate cover for deer to travel between feeding and bedding areas.

➢ Saddles (passes) in mountain ranges - Again, deer take paths of least resistance. If there's thick cover on one end of a saddle and, say, a farmer's field on the other, there's certain to be good hunting somewhere through the saddle, if there's a good deer population in the area. Saddles also funnel trails running with the hill on either or both ends of the saddle.

➢ Holes/breaks in fences - Again, deer take the path of least resistance. Adult deer can jump a five-strand barbwire fence without a running jump, but they prefer to use a hole, or low place, if it is available, unless they are spooked. Fawns will normally "belly out" and go under a fence. Fawns can squeeze through rather small holes. After a fawn is about five months old, they too can jump a rather high fence, but mom will cross at a hole or low place so her fawn can easily follow.

Look for hair on barbwire barbs at holes, low places in fences, and places where the fence goes across a low spot in the terrain. If a deer jumps a fence, its under parts may drag across the barbs, leaving white hair on the barbs, as pictured below. If a deer crawls through a hole in a fence, or under a fence, its back may drag across barbs, leaving dark hair on the barbs.

➢ Man made funnels - You can actually create funnels by cutting holes in a good high fence or loosening the top strands of wire to make a low place. I don't recommend doing this unless it's your fence. You can also create funnels by clearing a path through areas of thick cover. This should be done weeks, or even months, prior to hunting the area. Your path should run the same direction as existing trails, which normally run between bedding and feeding areas, and should run with any slopes. You could increase traffic on these paths by falling trees, piling brush, etc. across any adjacent natural trails.

➢ Low places in bluffs - Deer love to travel bluffs after a little hunting pressure. There's no human scent down there. You'd be surprised how steep a bluff a deer can comfortably travel. They enter and leave at low places along the bluff and/or where a big gully enters the bluff.

➢ Dry spot between/in swampy areas - This is an ideal bedding spot; therefore, this spot may be a dandy morning stand.

➢ Watering holes - If the weather has been dry, the watering hole (small pond, spring, etc.) has good cover, and there's thick growth nearby, you may have a good stand. Deer must have water once or twice per day, but can normally satisfy this need using mud puddles and water in rock crevices as they browse, going to and from their primary feeding areas. Articles have been written on how great stands are at watering holes. This may be true in desert like areas. My experience says they are only good during a long dry period and have good cover, and only then in late evening on their way to primary feeding areas.

➢ Fox squirrel (large, slow, awkward squirrel that may be gray, black, brown, white, or some combination of these colors) and/or heavy chipmunk populations seem to have a strong correlation with heavy deer populations. A concentration of mast attracts all nut eaters.

➢ Look for sunny sides of hills and conifer groves in low areas if the wind chill is below twenty degrees Fahrenheit. Also, on windy days look for windbreaks created by the terrain and/or conifer groves. Some spots are sheltered from the winds.

➢ Adjacent and downwind of thick cover (bedding areas) may have potential of having a good stand location. Several other transitions points seem to attract whitetail: Transitions between different vegetations (fields to woods, open woods to clear cuts, etc.) and between different terrains (flat land to steep hills, dry land to swamps, etc.).

❖ Reading Sign

Trails - Train your eye to see straight lines of compacted leaves. Where an old log crosses a deer trail, the log will be beaten away from the deer's hooves hitting it. Where a trail goes down a short steep slope, the trail may be at least partly to dirt and you should see sliding marks and/or hoof rakes. Don't expect a deer trail to be deep and muddy. Sometimes a trail will be so barely visible that most hunters will walk over it and never see it, including myself if I do not have my mind on reading sign at that moment. Sometimes the light, filtering through the canopy of tree growth, must be at a certain angle to see one. As leaves are falling, and until a good rain after they fall, it's hard to see trails. Unless your eyes are better than mine, you should check for trails just before the leaves start falling. Look for more than one trail coming close enough together that you can cover them all from your lofty perch using your bow or gun. Better yet, look for two or more trails intersected by still another trail. If you are a gambler, I don't have to tell you what this does to your odds of seeing deer from your stand. Big bucks may make faint trails near (and normally just above) heavy trails. Don't confuse a beaver trail, coming out of a creek or branch, with a deer trail. Make sure that the trail is on both sides of the creek/branch. Make sure you actually see deer tracks in this case. Walk up or down hills. Deer travel along a hill, and seldom will go up and down. By walking up or down a hill you should get a good cross-section of deer travel along the hill. You will find deer trails in pastures, semi-grown up pastures, brier thickets, pines, young hardwoods, big hardwoods, recent clear-cuts, old clear-cuts, etc. Some of these trails are primarily night travel trails (close to primary feeding areas and/or areas with poor cover). As a rule of thumb, you'll normally find trophies (and old does) in or around thick growth, three feet high or higher, especially after the deciduous leaves fall and deer get a little hunting pressure. I've seen a lot of exceptions to this rule. Rut may cause a trophy to take off across an open pasture after a doe in heat. A spooked trophy is very likely to take off across an open pasture also. If a field has begun to grow up, a buck may take a shortcut through it during daylight.

Feeding Sign - Whitetails paw to uncover acorns, mushrooms, etc. beneath the leaves/needles. The sign of whitetail pawing for food should not be confused with turkeys scratching for acorns. The whitetail will leave paw rakes, with a small pile of leaves at one end. You may also see some partial acorns that have fallen from the deer's mouth and/or some deer droppings. Look for tops eaten off small trees, vines, and bushes. If the woody ends are still white it's fresh. Hedge apples and other fruits may be found burst open by the deer's hoofs or may be nibbled on. Heavy feeding sign, found near thick cover, may mean that the whitetail are using the feeding spot for their midday snack, and, if so, may make a dandy stand location.

Beds - Leaves, grass, or needles being flat and compact in an oval area, compared to the surrounding area, is probably a deer bed. If one is warm, when found, you ran it out as you walked into the area. Finding actual beds confirm that you have found a bedding area. Beds can tell you the size of the deer, which may give an indication of whether it is a buck or doe. If the leaves are roughed at one end, it is probably a buck. Bucks sometimes "doodle" with their horns while bedding. I've actually watched bucks do this. If there are one or two small beds nearby, it's a doe with her fawns and she has not yet gone into heat. During early season, while leaves are still on deciduous trees and undergrowth, deer are more spread out. After leaves fall, deer beds will normally be found in clear-cuts, cedar thickets, difficult to get to bluff type areas, etc., especially if hunting pressure is heavy.

Scrapes (pawed spots made by bucks) - You should begin to see scrapes sometime near mid October. Look for scrapes near deer trails, in logging roads, small clearings within good cover, adjacent to or at the edge of fields, in thickets, etc. Don't confuse scrapes with turkey scratching. If there are turkeys in the area, look around and see if there are numerous scratched spots. If so, it's probably turkey scratching. Scrapes will go to dirt and often have a shallow rut or two made by hoofs going down through the scrape area. Scrapes may be damp from urine and/or have a big deer track in it. You may smell the urine odor also. Don't confuse scrapes with feeding pawing. Scrapes are more defined than when they paw for food. Scrapes are a good potential stand most anywhere you may find them. If there are no leaves/needles in the scrape, it is fresh. Give higher priority to scrapes with overhanging branches, vines, or new growth that have been thrashed and/or chewed on. Inspect these branches for broken twigs and skinned bark, resulting from the buck horning and/or chewing the limb to leave his signature scent. See Chapter One under "Whitetail Vulnerabilities - Food and Sex".

Rubs (horning sign made by bucks) - Look for fresh rubs near trails, logging roads, feeding areas, and bedding areas. Rubs are easy to recognize. Sometimes you can spot them from your vehicle, as you drive through hunting areas. The rubbed area will normally be on one side of the tree or sapling. You can get an idea of how big a rack that a buck has from rubs. A two-inch diameter oak, cedar, etc. twisted off and lying nearby, says that you've got a big one. A tree or bush with some branches skinned or broken, says that it has got to be at least a four-point. A straight and pencil size sapling rubbed, doesn't necessarily mean that it was a spike. Any size buck may rub one like this occasionally. Look for prior year rubs, also. If a buck traveled there last year, most likely, the same buck, or another, will do the same this year. Old rubs are especially helpful when hunting an unfamiliar area in early season. A "rub line" is a long row of rubbed bushes/saplings, old or new, clearly defining an established buck trail. Don't be tempted to pick a stand near rubs, unless they are near potential bedding areas. A location, along this trail, a short distance from bedding, may make a dandy stand, if you position where your scent trail will not drift toward the approaching buck. You will not always find rubs or scrapes near a buck's bedding area. One of the best bucks I've killed had no rubs or scrapes that I could find. Do not forget that rub making declines, or even stops, about early November after bucks have established status/dominance. Not realizing this point could make a hunter think that his buck has relocated or been killed. See Chapter One under "Whitetail Vulnerabilities - Food and Sex".

Whitetail droppings - As you scout, look for droppings. They can tell you what has been there and when it was there. What was there? Small elliptical manure nodules, rather scattered, means it was a fawn. Fawn droppings may also be small nodules molded together forming "turds". Large/medium elliptical manure nodules, rather scattered, means it was a doe or yearling buck. Large manure nodules molded together in the form of a pile or "turd" may mean it's a buck or an exceptionally big doe. Some hunters say solid "turds" may be the result of the forage they are eating and/or the time of year. When was it dropped? Steaming means that it happened minutes ago. Wet, soft, green colored, and shiny nodules mean that it is only hours old. It hasn't had time to dry. Dry, black colored, and normal shape means anything from hours to days old, depending on when it last rained. If you can barely tell that it is deer manure, this means that it was dropped prior to the last rain.

Tracks - Slick/shiny mud, where it slid, means that it's fresh. It may be minutes or hours old. If it rained hard last night and the tracks are distinct, they're fresh (made since the rain). If upturned leaves are still damp, they are fresh. A mature doe and a young buck have similar tracks. A trophy buck will have tracks at least 3 1/2 inches long and fatter than that of a doe or young buck. The tracks of an old trophy buck may show signs of its hooves being chipped/cracked. Dewclaws behind the track say it's a big deer and probably a buck. Some hunters say a buck makes spread hoof tracks – I've not seen evidence to substantiate this.

❖ Scouting - The more human scent/sounds/sightings a deer detects, the more nocturnal they become (especially trophy bucks and older does) and the more they tend to travel/feed in thick cover. When scouting, wear rubber boots or "pacs", don't touch bushes, etc. as you walk, and don't spit, smoke, etc. Don't talk, clang metal, or make other obvious human sounds (and hope other hunters, scouting the area, do the same). Scout just enough to learn what you must. Additional scouting will spook deer unnecessarily.

Late winter to spring scouting - Look for antler sheds. Bucks start shedding their racks in mid to late January. Finding a rack shed tells you (1) that the buck made it through hunting season alive, (2) the rack size he'll probably be carrying next whitetail season and (3) where he resides. Rodents will probably have eaten these antler sheds if you wait until fall to scout. If you're a turkey hunter, try scouting for antler sheds while turkey hunting. Look for antler sheds in and around bedding/feeding areas. By spring turkey season the sheds will probably be bleached white, and will resemble a pile of bones. Late winter to spring is a good time to scout unfamiliar hunting areas. You can see much further in the woods, with the leaves off of the deciduous trees, which allows you to find saddles, gullies, benches, and other "funnels", as well as old "rub lines", etc., much easier. Follow the "rub line" toward his probable bedding area and you'll likely have a nice stand for next fall. Ticks, chiggers, snakes, etc. are less of a problem then also. Some articles tell us to do all scouting in the late winter to spring to avoid spooking whitetail prior to hunting. But, deer movement will probably change some before you start hunting in the fall. Unless you've hunted the area in prior years, and know what to expect, scout just days before you intend to hunt the area. Clear cutting, food supply changes, etc. will change deer travel from one year to the next. Deer may change their travel habits after the leaves fall and they lose cover. Under a particular white oak that was pawed to pieces last year may not draw any attention this year. They may have found something better, closer, or whatever this year. Once the first shot is fired they may change bedding areas. Also, once the rut begins, a good buck may travel to new areas to find does in heat.

Try to determine where deer are probably bedding and where they are probably feeding. This one-way trip may be as far as five miles (some say ten miles but, if this is true, it's rare, and if they do, they may spend days/weeks before returning) or as short as a few hundred yards. This is why you'll normally find heavy beaten trails near the primary feeding area, and these trails will branch out, becoming more faint, farther from the feeding area. Occasionally, you'll find heavy trails entering a bedding area (thick growth). This makes a good stand, if the wind is favorable and your scent trail, therefore, controllable.

If livestock have access to wooded areas or grownup pastures, don't assume that the livestock made the trails. Deer may be traveling the trails also. Look for sign in the "funnel" areas outlined above. Look for old, out-of-service, permanent tree stands. Quite often the builder knew how to spot a good stand location.

When hunting the same general area for an extended time, try to do a little walk through scouting about once per week. Do this as you walk out from the morning hunt and back in for the evening hunt, if possible, to minimize spreading human scent unnecessarily.

❖ Unfamiliar Areas - You've decided to go to a Wildlife Management Area that you've never been to. Get a map from of the WMA you plan to hunt, and go scout it a week or so before the hunt. Determine the general area to hunt. Have two or three alternates in case other hunters overrun you. Look for heavy trails on banks, along the road, as you drive through your new areas. This can indicate deer population and tell you where they are feeding and/or bedding. Don't forget that other hunters can easily see road sign also. Follow these trails toward the thick growth bedding area to find a good stand. Look for saddles, benches along hills, a patch of oaks in the middle of a clear-cut, large gullies, etc. outlined in "Funnel Them to You" above. Concentrate on areas that you think fewer hunters will be attracted to, even if it appears to have less deer sign. Deer escape routes are probably your best bet. Look for trails leading into clear cuts, saddles, low places in bluffs, trails entering swamps, narrow places in a large area of good cover and ends of slews. Ride around your chosen areas, looking for the closest primary feeding area. This may give you an idea of the time of day they will be entering/leaving the bedding area. Now, plot all this information on a map and determine deer travel with respect to your chosen area or escape routes to hunt. Then, start looking for detailed sign, and specific stands you can hunt from, preferably close to thick cover and other potential escape routes.

You just got permission to hunt a farm with fields and woods. In this scenario, deer travel will probably not be altered by undue human scent/sounds/sightings, and the sign that you read will be more meaningful. Determine the primary feeding and bedding areas as soon as possible. Map the area to help determine deer travel patterns. Include general terrain, fences, roads, logging roads, fields, bluffs, streams, ponds, etc. Note feeding area, bedding locations, and general travel between them. Note heavy scrape and "rub lines". Note deer sightings and their travel directions. Find the funnels as soon as possible (See "Funnel Them to You" above). Find the trails around the bedding areas. Plot this information on your map also. Now, study the map to determine possible routes your buck could be traveling to and from bedding, and where the best stand locations will be. Note normal wind directions at these spots. See the sample map below.

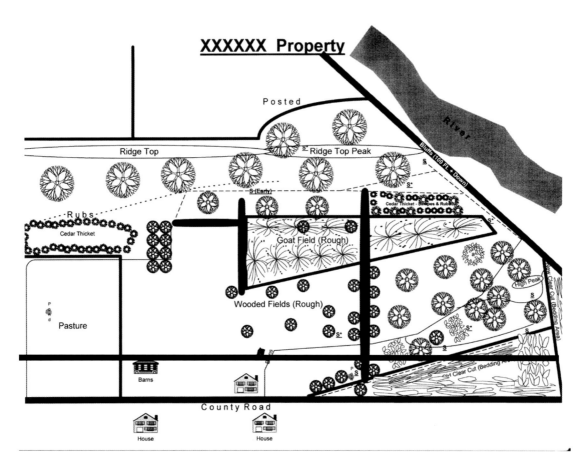

❖ Controlling Your Scent Trail - "Scent trail" is the pattern in which the air currents carry a hunter's odors, as they move downwind from the hunter. The concept of controlling the scent trail is a VERY IMPORTANT part of becoming a highly skilled whitetail hunter, since the whitetails sense of smell is so acute.

Selecting your stand downwind (or at least not upwind) of where you expect the deer to come through is your best scent control ploy. You should monitor your potential stand for as long as an hour, studying the wind direction, and making sure that it doesn't switch directions excessively. Air currents do strange things in mountainous terrain, but some spots are better than others. Select your stand as far away from the trail that the deer should follow, as your shooting device allows. This way if the wind shifts momentarily, your deer may not smell you. During archery season, this distance is limited to twenty to thirty yards, shotguns may allow forty to fifty yards, but the muzzleloader and rifle hunter can move fifty to a hundred yards away, depending on visibility and your shooting ability.

Wind fanning - Don't ignore the fanning effect of your scent. It fans in both the vertical and horizontal directions. At your body, your scent trail is only about two feet wide and six feet high; but fifty yards downwind; your scent trail may be twenty yards or more wide and high, depending on the wind speed. This means that a deer may walk around your tree and not smell you; but if it is twenty to thirty yards out (and downwind of you) it probably will.

Vertical currents - Thermal currents normally rise in the morning and descend in the evening, but there are lots of exceptions to this rule. Staying high on the hill from your deer trail in the morning is normally a safe decision, especially if the general wind direction is going up hill at some angle. Stay down the hill from a good trail in the evening, as a rule, but monitor the wind direction to make sure this rule is correct for your stand location (lots of exceptions to this rule). Falling barometer precedes most fall storms. During this time, your scent may tend to go down, just as smoke from a chimney tends to go toward the ground, as a front moves through an area.

Wind direction - Don't ever expect the wind to blow precisely in the same direction all of the time. Even in the best cases, the wind will sweep one way then the other to some degree. In mountainous terrain, air currents can do tricky things. Its direction can be very unpredictable, on a given day, and may switch directions frequently. Some places, within a hunting area, will have more stable air currents than others. I've been on stands where the wind actually reversed directions routinely. Positioning your stand higher on the hill/mountain seems to help control your scent trail, especially in the morning. Even if the wind is going in the downhill direction, in the morning, thermal currents may keep your scent above the trail that you are watching, especially if you are twenty-five feet up a tree. The only sure wind test is to spend time on the stand. If it switches terribly and/or goes the wrong direction on a day of normal weather, find another stand. I've quit using, otherwise, outstanding stands purely on the basis of scent trail control.

❖ Picking Tree for Portable Tree Stand - If you are using a portable tree stand, pick a tree to accommodate your stand safely - not too big, not too small, not leaning too much, etc. Pick a tree having no lower limbs or be prepared to cut some limbs on your first trip up the tree. Folding saws work well for this task. The tree must be downwind from the area that you expect the deer to come to you. Pick a tree that has some neighboring foliage that will give you some cover if you can. This is seldom possible, but is a plus. The tree should be as far away from the point you expect the deer to come through as you can accurately shoot to. Pick a tree that disallows the sun being in your eyes if practical. It's near impossible to satisfy all "wants" and this "want" is less important than the above. Having the sun to your back is a disadvantage if it casts a shadow to the ground, where it would allow an approaching deer to see shadow movements as you move into shooting position.

During archery season, saplings/limbs/brush can easily deflect your arrow. Bullets can also be deflected if they hit a woody growth. Minimize the possibility of bullet/arrow deflection. Make shooting lanes by bending saplings/limbs/brush from a direct line-of-sight from your planned shooting position, to the spot you expect deer to enter your area. Cut them if you must but cutting too many will cause the deer to quit using the trail. If you have no choice but to make shooting lanes by cutting saplings, do it at least a week prior to the hunt and don't disturb the saplings/limbs/brush any more than you must.

❖ Permanent Tree Stands - I strongly discourage using them. They are unsafe, even if you personally built them out of treated lumber and galvanized coated ring shank nails. As years go by, they deteriorate. As the wind moves the tree, the connections become loose. Molds, mildew, etc. grow on the boards making them very slick when damp or wet. A layer of frost or ice on the boards is even worse. I've had a close call or two using them. All articles that I've read, regarding permanent stands, agree that we should not use them. They are inflexible. If the wind changes or the deer movement changes, you can't pick it up and relocate it. If used routinely, mature bucks will avoid the area of the permanent stand. If you do use them, the same points are appropriate for picking permanent stands locations as for portable tree stands. You should not waste time and money building a permanent stands until you've hunted the area for a season or two and learn the deer's travel patterns. They are not legal in most Wildlife Management Areas. I'd frown on you building one on my property too. They damage or even destroy trees. Saw-millers may refuse to saw a log if they are aware that the tree had a stand built in it. The saw blade hitting nails is dangerous and expensive.

❖ Picking Your Ground Blind Location - The same points for picking portable tree stand locations are also appropriate for picking ground blind locations. You may be lucky enough to find a large tree lap to crawl into. You may cut cedars and form a circle or semicircle. Deep holes from uprooted trees, etc. work well also. I've even seen ground blinds built out of branches by forming a crude log house. Or, you can use two or three tree umbrellas and surround yourself. In this case you can wait until the time you start hunting the spot to erect your blind. This method gives you good flexibility. Note the following photo.

Setup Using Two Tree Umbrellas

Tent type ground blinds are also available. They too provide good flexibility.

Chapter Six
Stand Hunting - Getting to Your Stand

This chapter is intended to give you a few pointers between getting out of bed to when you get to your stand. Most hunters give little thought to this part of the hunt, but it can have a very significant impact on how many deer you see during the day. So, the weekend is finally here. The big day you've been waiting for all week is almost here.

❖ From Bed to Hunting Area - Get to bed early and get enough sleep for your body's need. When you go to bed and roll and tumble, because you're excited about your Saturday hunt, get up and find a sleeping pill, glass of milk or whatever. No sleep at night means that you may go to sleep on your stand the next day. Have a reliable alarm clock and don't forget to set it. When you wake up, take your shower, using no-odor soap, dab on some no-odor underarm deodorant, and don't shave. A day's beard growth reduces light reflecting from your face and no shaving lotion reduces odor the deer will smell. (See Chapter Seven under "Minimize your body scent") Dress to the day's weather. What's the temperature? Check it before you start dressing and dress accordingly. Dress in layers. This is especially important if you plan to drive or still hunt at midday. Know how much clothing you need for a given temperature range. Wear rubber boots or "pacs" to reduce your trail odors, which a deer may smell for up to two hours. Is it going to rain? Do I need to wear or carry a rain suit? Carry a tree umbrella. It's good to mount them on your tree even if it's not going to rain. A deer looking up at you may silhouette you against the sky and movements are magnified.

If you drive through a nice pasture an hour before daylight, get out of your truck, get ready, and walk into the woods (probably using the same trail that your deer are using) you are not going to see many deer at your stand and certainly not the shrewd old buck. Consider using another direction or abandoning the spot altogether. Before walking in, consider scent control (wind direction and thermal currents, etc.). Ask yourself, "Will my scent drift in a direction that will drive the deer out as I walk in". Have an alternant route, even if it is a longer walk, that will not allow your scent trail to drift through the area that you will be hunting. Consider hunting an alternant stand for that day if the wind direction is unfavorable. Do you need to urinate or defecate? It's better to spread this scent at your vehicle than in the woods near your stand. It may be a good idea to spread some wax type doe-in-rut scent on your boots in case you dribbled on them or otherwise picked up some human scents. Some hunters make a point of stepping in "cow piles", or some other natural scent, as they walk in. Some hunters tie scent bags to their boots or drag them on a string. Some hunters lace the back leg scent glands, of a recent deer kill, into their bootlaces.

❖ From Vehicle to Stand - Keep your bearings while you are walking to your morning stand. Don't spread scent all over the area, while trying to find your stand in the dark. Use fences, creeks, lakes, bluffs, mountain skylines, trees, towers, logging roads, etc. to help you stay on course. I have noticed that deer hunters who have coon or fox hunted have less trouble maintaining their bearings in darkness than those who have little experience navigating dark wooded terrain. They have become masters at reading these natural landmarks. If necessary mark the trail using surveyor's ribbon, bright-eyes (tacks with fluorescent plastic on the head), etc. I use them occasionally, when hunting unfamiliar areas with few landmarks that I can see in the dark. Realize that other hunters may follow these markers to your stand also. For this reason, do not use them unless you have to. If you have a real problem finding your spot, consider waiting until first light to walk in. Occasionally I hear a hunter say, "I never get turned around in the woods". I always want to ask them if they've been in transit to or from a stand a mile or so deep in darkness, in flat unfamiliar territory, with no logging roads, fences, creeks, etc. to stay on course and a good thick fog. Mother Nature can cook up some panicking situations sometimes. Carry a compass, and don't forget to check your entry direction, before leaving your vehicle. Draw a map and file it for future hunts. Or, use a global positioning system (GPS) device. They receive a signal from one of several different satellites circling the earth, referring to the exact longitude and latitude of your position, giving your precise location anywhere in the world. It is, by far, the most advanced and accurate positioning and navigation system available to hunters.

If you're carrying a tree stand and you hear it making a noise, the deer can too. Stop and solve the noise problem. Don't touch twigs, branches, etc. as you walk in. Deer can smell the oils from your skin, which you leave when you touch something, for hours. Do not use a big light to walk to your morning stand. How far can a deer see a light? Carry the smallest AA flashlight that you can find your stand with. It's light, compact, and doesn't spook the whitetail unnecessarily. If safety allows try not using a light. Carry your coat. If you break a heavy sweat walking to your stand, you can chill while sitting still at your stand, even if the temperature is as high as fifty degrees Fahrenheit. You'll also spread more human scent for the rest of the day after you break a heavy sweat. Put your coat on before you start up your tree or sit down at your ground blind. Don't wait until you get cold to put it on. By this time, you've lost too much body heat and may chill. Using a utility vest with a large game pouch, allows you to stuff your coat in it, leaving your hands free, as you walk to/from your stand, to carry your shooting device.

❖ When You Get to Your Stand Location - Place a few drops of Tink's Doe Pee (or, if rut has begun, Tink's #69 Doe-In-Rut Pee) or equivalent on each side of your scent trail and as far from your stand as you will easily see and shoot to. If you think the wind may switch, place it on all four sides of your stand. Hopefully the deer will smell the lure scent trail, before moving into your scent trail, and divert toward the lure scent trail; thus, missing your scent trail. If you are using a portable tree stand, place your stand on the tree, if you haven't previously done so. Don't forget to tie your weapon to your pull-up cord. Buckle your safety belt to you so you will not have to do it in the tree. How high should you go in your lofty perch? Twenty to twenty-five feet (20'-25') should do the job. If you are using a ground blind, crawl into your fallen tree, place tree umbrellas in a semicircle around you, or erect your tent blind. If you are using a compound bow or crossbow, tie surveyor ribbon at three or four locations around your tree or ground blind at whatever distance your bow will shoot a near flat trajectory. Doing so will avoid guessing at distance, up to this point, unnecessarily.

Chapter Seven
Stand Hunting - At Your Stand

Now you are ready to reap the benefits of the time you spent selecting the correct hunting area, scoutings, finding just the right stand locations, etc. This is the fun part. Don't "blow" it now!
❖ Scent Control

Luring scents - This is a spray solution, wax, spray powders, or bottle solutions of actual or man-made doe pee or doe in estrus pee. Do not use an applicator that requires that you handle it and place it somewhere. The deer may smell your scent and vamoose. I use a pump spray applicator. You can also find it in wax form in a roll-up applicator. These work well on a wet day. Use doe pee prior to the rut and doe in rut pee during the rut. Placing it around your stand location may divert deer to it before they enter your scent trail and spook.

Scent neutralizers - This is a spray bottle solution that you spray on your clothing before you go into the woods. It is sold to neutralize the human odor, so the deer down wind will not smell you. It helps, but do not depend on it to eliminate all of your scent.

Masking scents - This is a spray bottle solution that you spray on your clothing or it may come in a bottle that requires you to dab on when you get to your stand. It is sold to over power, or masks, the human odor so the deer down wind will not smell you. It may be skunk, fox, or coon scent or apple, acorn, cedar, pine, or earth scent. I recommend not using skunk scent – YOUR FAMILY WILL ALSO. I used it one year and felt that I saw fewer deer. I've read since then that, since a skunk sprays when distressed, deer may avoid an area when they smell it. Some hunters say it's the very scent to use, because it is so strong. Don't use masking scents not found in the area that you are hunting. If you use cedar scent and there is not a cedar tree for miles, deer may be spooked if they smell it. Masking scents help but do not depend on it to totally mask your scent.

Scent blocking suit (See Chapter Thirteen - "Clothing") - This is a garment aimed at locking in body odors, absorbing your odor, or reducing your odor causing bacteria growth. One that I use is charcoal impregnated fabric sandwiched between two layers of cloth. It seems to help but again do not be naive and think that the whitetail will not smell you. Scent-Lok brand makes head to toe systems. Cabela's offers outerwear that they advertise as having "total scent control" using a charcoal impregnated Scent-Lok lining. Supprescent brand is also used in outerwear garments to help suppress the hunter's scent.

Control scent trail - My first/primary defense for scent control is selecting the stand location properly, although I do use scent neutralizers and masking scents sometimes and luring scents routinely. Monitor the wind direction frequently. Close your eyes and try to feel the wind on your face. Which side of your face is cooler? Using a lighter works except it only gives you the wind direction at that moment. It doesn't give you a continuous indication. Watching the direction that leaves, fluffy seed, etc. fall to the ground gives a fair indication of air current direction. Tying a goose down feather to your gun or bow, using a fine string, should give you a continuous reading on wind direction. Select a stand that controls your scent. (See Chapter Five under "Control Your Scent Trail").

Minimize your body scent - Human scent can be smelled by a deer from a hundred yards to hundreds of yards, depending on just how much you stink to the deer. Some scent control efforts may seem ridiculous to some hunters; but, the more of it you can do, the better your odds of seeing deer. Early season hunting dictates the use of an insect repellant. The alternative is mosquito and gnat swatting motions, which hurts your odds of seeing deer more than the repellant scent. Or worse yet, get an infestation of ticks or chiggers that will keep you itching for days. Choose those repellants advertised to have "no scent", even though I'm sure deer can smell it. Take a bath at the beginning of each hunt day (use odorless soap) if you can. Do not use cologne or scented after shave or shaving lotion. Change under clothing daily. Change other clothing if they get sweat soaked or otherwise contaminated with deer alarming odor. Air your outerwear outside the night prior to your hunt. Better yet, stuff them in a plastic bag with pine needles and leaves. Do not smoke at your stand if possible. You may consider using chewing tobacco on your hunt days but spit in a bottle, not on the ground. If you must smoke, scent trail control measures should be exaggerated. Do not eat heavy garlic spiced foods or other spices that contribute to body odor. I heard of a hunter who didn't eat meat for a month prior or during the season. He believed that a deer could differentiate between the scent of a meat eater and a vegetarian and be scared of the meat eater. This may very well be true, but I'm not carrying scent control that far. Do not urinate or defecate in the woods if at all possible. Urine odor may linger in the woods for days. If you defecate in the woods, this odor must linger until the next hard rain, which could be weeks! Personally, I carry a bottled drink to my stand and use the empty bottle to urinate in. If I have to have a bowel movement in the woods, I go several hundred yards downwind of my area. I will overturn a big rock and place it back when I am done, or dig a hole in the ground and cover it up when I am done. Some hunters use wet towels to clean with to reduce their body odor. Don't forget to take your gun or bow when you have to go. If you're hunting an area that you don't intend to hunt for a while, consider using your urine or bowel movement to divert deer to you from an area out of your sight if the wind direction allows. Hunting in drizzle or rain reduces human scent if the wind is not switching or gusty. A hunter may use this point to their advantage when hunting a "hotspot", where approaching deer have historically smelled you. It seems to me that bucks often bed in areas where the wind switches routinely.

❖ Sound Control - A deer under your tree can actually hear you breathing, if your breathing is heavy or your lungs are bubbling a little. Try not to cough. If your coughing is caused by sinus drainage, take an antihistamine before leaving home and/or carry some with you. If you must cough, bring all of your body clothing up around your face and press both hands against your mouth. Cough once and no more than once. The more times you cough, or make any other noise, the more likely that deer will pinpoint your location and dodge you. Don't "hack"; rather, "heave" it out. The sharp "hacking" sound carries for a much farther distance. If you hear a loud helicopter fly over, an eighteen wheeler coming by on a nearby highway, etc., take advantage of the loud noise to do your coughing. Don't sneeze! There is no need to sneeze. When you feel a sneeze coming on, at the last second, place your finger under your nose and push. It goes away and you've got the same satisfaction as if you've sneezed. If you accidentally make sound, use your deer call and make two simple calls. This tells deer, in hearing distance, that all is OK. If a squirrel spots you and barks and whips its tail in anger, use your deer call and make two simple calls. Squirrels also bark at whitetails.

❖ Sight Control - Sight is the whitetail's third most reliable sense, but the whitetail sees movement very well; so, it's important to reduce your movements and make movements in slow motion. Even though a deer can't differentiate most colors, they are not blind. Good camouflage is an advantage but is a bit over-rated. You'll spend more money for the latest camouflage outfit and last years or the old originals may be just as good. Use a pattern resembling the area that you will be hunting, and consider using different patterns for pants and shirt/coat. Consider using 3-D camouflage just to improve the odds a bit, because improving the odds is important!

It is very important to know that deer can see the same washing detergent brighteners on clothing that hunters can only see with the aid of an ultraviolet light. Have you ever been at a nightclub and notice how the clothing of the people on the dance floor glowed? This glow is a result of ultraviolet light shining on the brighteners in the clothing. This means wash your outerwear hunting clothes in a detergent that has no brighteners. It's difficult to find this type detergent these days. I use Arm & Hammer Super Washing Soda. You can pay more for some hunter's detergent but this does the same job. Don't forget that new clothing materials may have brightener. Either shine them with an ultraviolet light to see if they glow, or wash your new outerwear in a detergent with no brighteners.

In reality you will occasionally move while sitting at your stand. You will not always see a deer approach. If you do not see a deer approach, it will likely "catch you" moving or hear you. Once you see/hear the deer, automatically freeze and stay frozen. If a deer does not smell or hear you, but think it sees you, it may do the move-and-I-gotcha and their tap dance acts. It's really entertaining. The deer, normally an older doe, will point you like a bird dog and gaze at you for seconds (it seems more like hours). Then, it will drop its head, as if it's going about its normal routine (expecting you to move). Then, up comes the head again for several seconds. It may raise and lower its head, trying to get a "fix" on you. It may do this several times. Now comes the tap dance. It will bounce up and come down on its front hoofs, or lift one foot at a time and hit the ground, while at the same time looking at you. By this time, it probably will decide that you just don't belong up there, snort, and run off. It may circle your tree, down wind, to see if it can smell you. But occasionally, just occasionally, it will decide that you are no threat and go on feeding, or whatever it was doing before it caught you moving.

- ❖ Change Stands Frequently. The more consecutive uses of a stand, the poorer your odds of seeing deer. The more you travel to a given stand and sit at this spot, the more deer will smell/hear/see you and begin to dodge your position. As a rule, spend only one or two day at a given spot, waiting a couple of days before using it again. Don't be predictable. Moving a few hundred yards may accomplish your objective. Only a real "hot-spot" may justify spending over two days at the same stand location. If you've done your homework properly, you should have several "hot-spots"; so, changing stands frequently should not force you to choose less productive spots as a stand. This point is especially true when you use deer calls. Day in and day out calling from the same location would make a buck think that his honey is chained to a tree. This would just not sound natural to a buck, or a doe either.
- ❖ Talking To Trophy Buck (Deer Calling Techniques) - Deer have the herd instinct. Their social behavior, as it relates to the rest of the herd, is important to deer. Deer communicate by body language. For example, noise in the air and quick movements means "I think I smell danger" and they all get nervous. Whitetails also communicate verbally via a rather limited vocabulary. Whitetail hunters can capitalize on this point and use calls to manipulate deer behavior. This is a VERY IMPORTANT part of becoming a highly skilled whitetail hunter. Using a good deer call and rattle correctly can make the difference between a fair hunter and a good hunter. Deer calls really work if done correctly. I've succeeded many times and I'm still learning. Realize though that there are certain situations when calls should not be used. Following are some of the deer's basic calls and how/when the hunter can use them to become a better hunter:
  - ➢ Contact calls - Begin most calling sessions using these calls and use them all season. These are social calls, used by both buck and doe throughout the season to seek companionship of other deer.
    - ■ Lost call says "I'm lost; where are you; come to me" and are given rather loud and in a series of one or two calls spaced twenty to thirty seconds apart. It is made on a Woods Wise Products, Breeding Bellow call by inhaling softly with one hand cupped over the tube end, then open and close the hand, making the pitch and volume rise and fall.

Calls last two seconds (n-n-N-A-A-A-A-a-h). Wait twenty to thirty minutes and repeat the series.

■ Buck/doe bleats are less intense calls that say simply "come " and are very short and soft. This call coaxes deer. It is made on a Woods Wise Products, Breeding Bellow call by inhaling softly for one-forth second bleats in a random two to four call sequence (n-a-a, pause n-a-a, etc.).

➢ Estrus bleat - This call is made by the doe and says, "I'm ready to be bred", but can be used throughout the season and with the peak rut courting ritual. Using a Breeding Bellow call device, this call is made by inhaling softly for about one second long "bleat" (n-n-a-a-a-h) and repeated randomly two to four times. Wait twenty to thirty minutes and repeat.

➢ Breeding bellow - Since some breeding begins a month prior to peak rut and continues for a month after peak rut, this call will work from about mid October through mid December. It works on all bucks, because all bucks are active in breeding to some degree. Unlike the aggressive grunts it will not spook lesser bucks. This call is made by the doe and says, "Come here immediately; I must be bred now". On a Breeding Bellow call, inhaling softly for about one-fourth second. Now, exhale rather forcefully for a one second brassy "bellow" (n-e-e-e/A-A-U-U-U-U-G-H). Wait twenty to thirty minutes and repeat. This call should be made sparingly; it can be easily overdone.

➢ Buck bawl - Bucks remain social with each other throughout the fall as long as a hot doe isn't involved. This call is a social "Here I am, come here" call. It is a low/raspy sound. The "buck bawl" is a buck association call that invites bucks to come and visit. There is no aggression involved in this call. Unlike the "grunt" calls (discussed below), that may cause other bucks to bristle up or become cautious, the "buck bawl" will cause the buck to walk to you calmly and may bring in less dominant bucks or one that just got beat-up on by another buck. This call is most appropriate for the hunter to use during early bow and late gun season, when bucks are tired and actively seek other bucks to socialize. It may also be effective if occasionally used during the rut period. The "buck bawl" works well with the "sparing" rattling call also. On the Breeding Bellow call, or most any "grunt" call, exhale softly into the call for one-half second with the tube extended and give random spaced single calls one to four times. Wait twenty to thirty minutes and repeat. It sounds like a calf bawl.

➢ Aggressive buck grunt - This call is the same as the "buck bawl" except it is about twice as long (one second) and louder. Use three or four "grunts" randomly spaced. Bucks begin making this sound as the rut approaches.

➢ Tending buck grunt - This call is similar to the aggressive "grunt". Make one-second "grunts", spaced three to six seconds apart, in a sequence of five to ten "grunts". Bucks make this sound when following/seeking a hot doe. Use this call predominately during the rut period for your area.

➢ Tending buck "pops" - The tending buck may occasionally make this sound while chasing the doe. It can be made on most grunt calls by saying "tuck" three to four times into the "grunt " call, "popping" air over the reed. Use this call sparingly, during peak rut, after using the "tending grunt" call.

➢ Tending hyperventilating buck grunt - A frustrated rutting buck may occasionally make this sound while chasing the doe. The call can be made on a double reed call, like the Knight & Hale EZ-Grunt-er "Plus", Model 1003. Use this call sparingly, during peak rut, after using the "tending grunt" call. Inhaling-exhaling, using a life-like rhythm, makes this call. Adjust the length of the tube to change the pitch of the grunts.

➢ Buck wheeze - A rut crazy buck, when confronted by rival bucks, may make this call. Bucks make this sound to intimidate other bucks and prevent fights. This call will run off all but the most dominate buck. A frustrated tending buck may make this sound while chasing the doe. Blowing air through the tube (removed from the call) of most "grunt" calls can make this sound. Simply press your lips rather tight together and blow blasts of air through the tube. Blow two to four blasts getting less forceful and taper off on the last. M.A.D Calls makes the Twist Tone and includes the "Snort Wheeze" tube in the package. The call sounds similar to letting air out of an automobile tire valve. Use this call sparingly and during peak rut.

➢ Sparring - All antlered bucks engage in some sparring in October. During September older bucks may even spar with young bucks. Rubbing real/simulated antlers together, a rattling bag, or an electronic/digital call makes this sound. Sparring calls may be appropriate throughout the hunting season. Use this call occasionally with any of the above calls, but use it rather sparingly and not over thirty seconds at once.

➢ Buck battle - During peak rut, two dominant bucks may do serious battle. Bucks may come to a good fight, since the result may impact their social dominance status in that area. "Buck battle" rattling calls are appropriate only during peak rut. The same call devices are used as with sparing but is much louder, faster, and aggressive.

➢ Fawns distress call - Some hunters use the fawn distress call in hopes of bringing a doe that may be separated from her fawn. This call is a long duration, high-pitched call. It sounds similar to a human baby crying. Personally, I avoid distress calls, because I think they make deer more cautious and avoid my area.

➢ Snort - This is the ultimate distress call used by all deer when they smell/hear/see anything threatening to them or theirs. A deer blowing forcefully through their nose makes the sound. Hunters should never use this sound as a call. Since it is the ultimate deer distress call, deer will avoid any area this call is sounded in.

➢ Miscellaneous calling - If I accidentally make a noise at my stand, I'll use a "buck/doe bleat" call or "buck bawl" to tell any deer that may be in hearing range that all is OK in my area. Otherwise, the deer may dodge my area. If a deer comes by out of shooting range or in thick cover where I can't get a shot, the "contact" calls may divert them in my direction. I've also had success using the "buck bawl" in this case. These calls should get his attention. Also, if you spook a deer, after it comes near your tree, using "contact" calls or the "buck bawl" may bring it back. You sure don't have anything to lose by trying. You'll be successful roughly thirty percent of the time. I once brought a big six point back into shooting range twice, for a young hunter, by using "buck bawls".

Following is an example of a sequence that could be used on a typical hunt session: Do the "contact lost call" once or twice. Wait twenty minutes and repeat. Do the "contact buck/doe bleat" two to five times with random spacing. Wait twenty to thirty minutes. Do the "buck bawl" a couple of times with random spacing. Wait twenty to thirty minutes. Do the "estrus bleat" two to four times with random spacing. Wait twenty to thirty minutes. Do the "estrus bleat" two to six times and add a "breeding-bellow" somewhere among the "estrus bleats". Use random spacing. Continue this call ever twenty to thirty minutes.

Following is an example of the peak rut courting ritual: This ritual is especially effective during peak rut. If you know that there is a good buck in the area, and the above call sequences fail to bring him to you, try the more aggressive ploy. Realize that this ploy will run off the less aggressive bucks (which may or may not have the nicest rack) or the ones that just got beat-up on by another buck. The whole idea here is to make your buck think that some other buck is coming into HIS territory, trying to seduce a doe. He's also motivated by the possibility of a new doe in estrus. During the evening hunt, start the call session with two or three "estrus bleats". Do this ever twenty to thirty minutes during the first hour at your stand. Next, do two to four "estrus bleat", with a "breeding bellow" mixed in. Do this ever twenty to thirty minutes for the next hour. Next, do the "estrus bleat" sequence, outlined above, immediately followed with an "aggressive buck grunt".   This simulates the buck having located the doe in heat.   Next, do the same, except make both doe calls more intense and choppy, and then do the "tending buck grunt" sequence. Do this once, about ten to twenty minutes before dark, and then wait until dark for the results. A very cautious buck may not come to you until right at dark. During the morning hunt, start calling just after daylight enough to shoot. I started too early one foggy morning, and a big deer came close, turned and left before I could confirm that it had horns. Once a buck sees no source for the call, he will normally leave rather quickly. Do two or three "estrus bleats" and a "breeding bellow", immediately followed with two or three "aggressive buck grunts". Occasionally use the "tending buck grunt" sequence. You may use the "buck battle" rattle call once for a few seconds. I use only the more aggressive calls in the morning because deer are moving toward their bedding area and I want to make sure that the buck on the move hears the more aggressive sequence at least once. Some hunters use this method in the evening also. About two hours after daylight, I try to do even more aggressive calling. The calls are more broken, louder, and longer.

Sometimes a buck or two may come within forty to sixty yards of your position and "hang up", refusing to come another foot. This is a real problem in archery season, when your maximum reliable shooting distance may not be over thirty yards. It's also a problem in gun season if you hunt in thick cover and/or the buck comes to you right at dark. Also, by gun season, bucks are much more cautious; so, rather than coming in to forty yards, they may only come in to sixty or seventy yards to look for the sound source. If you see a buck that has responded to your calling, but will not come into the open, wait until his head is down or behind a tree/bush and "estrus bleat" one time (softly). If he still will not come to your position, use the "breeding bellow" call one time (muffled). The "buck bawl" may also work.

Deer, like humans, are all different. The number of calls in a sequence, that is most effective, will vary from area to area. Also, during peak rut, you should be more aggressive with both the number of calls within a sequence, as well as the time between sequences. I've suggested that you perform the sequences ever twenty to thirty minutes in most cases. Some hunters and call manufacturers recommend using them more frequently. Your judgment will be required to set the exact time between the sequences.   The rut period for your area, is the most significant variable that you should consider to make this decision. Also, you could call more frequently during the last hour of daylight. It is better to error on the side of calling too infrequent and too few calls within a sequence than to call too frequently with too many calls within a sequence. Deer can become call-shy, relating the hunter's call to danger. Frequent calling is unnatural to the whitetail. Calling several days from the same stand is even more unnatural. If I plan to use the same stand location for a second day, I will call little or none on the first day. The more a hunter calls, the greater the odds of making a bad call (or making a call at an inappropriate time), and the more likely the deer will pinpoint your precise location and/or actually watch you make a call.

The proper volume for the circumstances is important. Low volume calls are normally more appropriate during bow season, and in areas that have heavy hunting pressure. If it is windy, during the rut, or if you don't get a response with low volume, increase the volume a bit. If you are not being successful, consider changing your call device. Remember, the buck may be walking along the trail, so all sounds being perfectly even is not natural. The calls that a deer makes, when walking, are slightly broken, rather than a long steady sound. Turn the grunt tube left and right slightly to simulate the buck moving his head. Cup your hand over the end occasionally forming a bugle. Stretch the call tube slightly and collapse it to simulate the deer's natural neck movement as they move along the trail. Point it toward the ground most of the time. To the listening deer, the sound should not sound like you are twenty-five feet up a tree and in one spot. Cup your hand over one side to "throw' the sound to one side to make it more difficult for the deer to pinpoint your exact position. Below freezing, you must keep the reed in the caller(s) from freezing. Most calls use a reed device to produce the sound. If the reed freezes and sticks to the rest of the call, it will probably make no sound and may produce some strange noise that could spook the deer. If the temperature is below freezing, keep the call(s) under your coat.

Deer sometimes need confirmation before coming close to a call source, especially if they do not see the source for the call and/or they smelled/heard/saw something that spook them. One late archery season hunt session, while twenty-five feet up a tree and using "estrus bleats" and "breeding bellows", I heard something to my rear, which was downwind. I eased around just in time to see a four-point buck, through the very thick undergrowth, stick his nose in the air, snort once, and run back up the hill. I called another call sequence of "estrus bleats" and a "breeding bellow", and no response. Now this buck came to my call and saw no doe as well as thought that he smelled me, so I sat back down in disgust. About thirty minutes later I was hungry and reached into my utility vest and pulled out a zip-lock bag of cashew nuts. As I dug for the nuts the cold plastic sounded like leaves crunching, but I was hungry and started chomping my cashews. Within seconds, the four-point trotted back down the hill and slid to a stop under my tree and right in the middle of the only opening in the underbrush on my back side. He heard confirmation sounds of, what he thought was, his doe walking in leaves (rattle of my plastic zip-lock bag) and her chomping on acorns (me chomping on cashews). Confirmation can be smell, sound, or sight. I learned something from this experience. Now I carry a sheet of plastic wrap that "crackles", like leaves crunching, when I move it. Digital calls have walking and feeding sounds at the touch of a button. I guess, just for illustrative purposes, if a hunter were willing to (1) tote in a full doe deer body mount and place it near big scrapes, (2) use a digital call with a remote speaker and place the speaker at the mount, (3) pour a couple of bottles of Tink's #69 doe-in-rut buck lure over the doe mount, and (4) play sounds of a deer crunching leaves and chomping acorns, along with trashy doe talk, that hunter would have some action before too long.

Know when NOT to use the calls. In areas where the buck to doe ratio is one to four or higher, bucks are not as motivated to come to a call. Heavily hunted deer and/or those very nocturnal bucks possibly will not come to a call in daylight hours. Therefore, if you are not getting expected responses on your calls, either find another hunting spot or consider not using the call or using them very sparingly. For best results, only call or rattle when hunting from a tree stand. When calling, you tell deer exactly where you are located. Deer can normally pinpoint sounds to within a few yards, especially if they hear the sound repeatedly, and/or they are a short distance from the source. When a deer responds aggressively to your call, it may come in quickly, so if you are hunting on the ground, they may see/smell/hear you or catch you unprepared. Even when correctly using a call from a tree stand, a deer may see your slow motion movement, because you've told them exactly where you are by calling. For this reason, deer calls are not the "magic bullet". I had a spike once come under my tree, looked all around for the source of the call and then looked straight up at me. He was so sure that the call source was located there that he looked up. Now, the trophy buck, or the older doe traveling with the buck, probably will not come to your tree. Rather, they will slip in and study you at fifty or more yards, probably near dark. They may stare intently at your position for over twenty minutes and if you move a muscle it will see you. You may see it or you may not. If you do see it, you may only get glimpses of it or you may see it when it starts bobbing its head up and down to get a "fix" on you. If this happens to you, relocate your stand, because you doubtfully will see the buck there for a while. Also, in thick cover you may be making a call while the buck watches you. My points here are: (1) To reduce the risk of a deer seeing you, look all around before making any call, (2) Do not use your calls if you're quite sure a buck is going to be traveling through anyway, (3) If you are hunting in thick cover, consider not calling, (4) Try to select a stand that has some obstruction, that a doe could logically be behind (in the mind of the buck), as he approaches, and (5) Consider, in some cases, just calling one sequence to get the buck headed your way, because the further away he is the less accurate his "fix" on your position will be.

You do not always know if you've performed the calling correctly. If a deer did not come to you did you do it wrong, no deer heard you, call-shy, saw no source for the calls and left, too many does per buck in the area, or sneaked in and smelled/saw/heard something unnatural and vamoosed. If a deer comes to you, would it have come anyway? Normally this answer is more obvious. Bucks seldom respond the same to calling. Some come running in, ready to do battle, especially when using the "peak rut courting ritual", some casually walk in, especially if expecting a friendly situation, and many sneak in, taking a few steps at a time. Still others will circle you, trying to pick up a scent trail. The ones that sneak and circle, you may never see. Following are some reality examples:

➢ Two eight points during morning session of early bow season - After using "contact calls" and "buck bawls", I observed two nice looking bucks circling my elevated position, while staying in good cover. They did a "show-off" antler-fencing thing, stared in my direction for several minutes, and then turned and began walking off. I used my rattling bag "sparring" call and one buck ran back toward me and stared, not moving a muscle, for at least twenty minutes, refusing to move close enough for me to get a shot. In this case, it was obvious to me that the bucks did not come any closer than forty yards to my elevated position, because they saw no source for the calls/rattling.

➢ Four-point morning kill in mid November - I started using the morning "peak rut courting ritual" just after daybreak. I used the rattle bag once about an hour after daylight for about thirty seconds, followed by an "aggressive buck grunt" and continued using the courting ritual. About three and one-half hours after daylight, the four-point, and his harem of three does, trotted under my tree, slid to a stop, and started looking around. As I moved into shooting position, the four-point looked at me twice. I stopped my movement each time but still, under non-rut conditions, he would have probably spotted me and bolted. After I shot, the does still hung around for about thirty seconds. All this tells me that I must have done the call correctly.

➢ Seven-point evening kill in late November - I started calling about three hours before dark. I used the evening "peak rut courting ritual" routine outlined above. At sixty minutes before dark I heard a squirrel bark about two hundred yards away and wondered if it could possibly be my buck. I started doing a very excited call sequence. At thirty minutes before dark the seven-point charged by me and stopped about thirty yards past me in thick cover. I assume he misjudged my location, which is very unusual. I did the "buck bawl" twice and he moved into the open. That was his last mistake. Since he ran past me, I had considerable movement getting into shooting position, and he did not see or hear my movements. All this tells me that I must have done the call correctly.

❖ At Your Stand Pointers
  ➢ Ask yourself, as you sit on your stand, "If I hunt here again do I need to relocate slightly to better control my scent trail, have better visibility, etc.". Also, study the terrain, review the sign that you've found to date, etc. and rethink how the deer could be traveling in the area.
  ➢ Constantly scan the woods for movements, colors that don't belong, and deer body parts. By the time you see the whole deer, it will be so close it is more likely to see your movement, as you get into shooting position.

  ➢ Make all movements in slow motion! Move your eyes, rather than your head and body, as much as possible. This point cannot be over emphasized.
  ➢ Look all around you and pick out all of the shooting holes that you have available. Don't assume the deer will always come to you from the direction that you expect it to. Know where all the openings are, so you'll be prepared regardless of the direction it comes from.
  ➢ Don't be tempted to shoot squirrels, turkeys, grouse, etc. while at your stand. Doing so will reduce your odds of seeing your whitetail, and it may be illegal in your area.
  ➢ Some hunters use polarized, yellow shooting glasses to improve visibility in low light. The yellow brightens the image, while the polarization improves depth perception and reduces glare. Deer like to move in shadows and good cover. These glasses brighten these spots and give the hunter better visibility. I've found this point to be extremely helpful. Some hunters carry binoculars and scan the woods very slowly looking for deer

body parts. Binoculars are more important when hunting more open areas and/or you are not using a weapon with a scope on it.

➢ Some bow hunters wear face paint (or some type of veil) and camouflage mesh gloves to improve the odds of not being seen by the deer. Personally, I've not found this to be necessary, if hunting twenty to twenty-five feet up in a portable tree stand. I do try to have a day or more beard growth to reduce face shine.

➢ Learn to tell the difference between the sounds deer make, walking, versus that of human, squirrel, chipmunks, etc. Doing so will reduce your movement to check out sounds and, more importantly, reduce the risk of accidentally shooting another human in the woods.

➢ If you are using a weapon with a variable power scope, make sure it is turned to the lowest power, so it will give you the widest field of view. It's a lot easier to dial it up, if you need to see detail at a long distance, than it is to dial it down if you have a buck at thirty yards and you've got to minimize motions. Trying to find a deer in a scope dialed to nine can waste valuable milliseconds. Also, if the deer is close, your scope view may not include the whole deer body; thus, finding the kill zone may become more difficult. If your weapon is equipped with a scope, and it is cold and/or moist, keep the scope away from the warmth of your body or it will fog the outside of the lens. It's revolting to aim in on a nice buck and the scope lens be fogged. When you bring your weapon, equipped with a scope, to your shoulder on a cool day, don't exhale on the front lens or it may fog the lens and distort your visibility.

➢ Wear a hat with little or no bill. You are constantly scanning the woods for movements, etc. Deer see horizontal movements more readily than vertical movements, because horizontal movements are less common in the woods. Therefore, a long bill hat rotating back and forth will be seen by a deer more readily than a short or no bill hat. If you must have a hat with a bill, wear a full brim hat. Stocking caps (toboggans) produce the least horizontal motion of all headwear that I've used. A turkey hunter's camouflage baseball cap, having netting attached to the bill and bottom perimeter, works well, but distorts visibility some.

➢ Listen to the squirrels, chipmunks, and pileated woodpecker (big with red head) alarm calls. They may tell you when a deer is headed your way. Chipmunks and pileated woodpeckers lie a lot, but squirrels don't lie much. The pileated woodpeckers seem to lie more than chipmunks. They will all sound an alarm when a hawk or owl flies through. If a squirrel barks and shakes its tail a few yards away, and looking in your direction, don't assume that it is directing its anger to you (as they often do). There may be a deer to your rear that you cannot see. If you hear a squirrel barking at another location, make a mental note of where it is, and check it out when you leave your stand. The squirrel may be telling you where a better stand is. The deer may be coming through there.

➢ When you first hear/see a whitetail, start getting into position to shoot. The sooner the better. The closer it comes to you, the more likely it is that your movement and/or sounds will be detected. Move very slowly and don't get excited. Move when heads are down and/or behind trees, bushes, etc. More than one deer means you are more likely to be smelled/heard/seen. If your heart begins to beat fast and/or your breathing becomes labored (and noisy), take two or three deep breaths. This should calm you down. If at first glance you see a rack (especially a big rack), DON'T LOOK AT IT, or at least don't let yourself focus on the rack. You'll have plenty of time to count points while you're field dressing it. Allowing yourself to focus on the rack will (1) likely get you all shook-up, increasing the odds of your making a mistake, and (2) may steal valuable milliseconds that you need before it smells/hears/sees you and bolts or moves out of your shooting lane.

➢ An adult doe traveling alone and rather fast is probably in heat and there's likely a buck behind her. She may even stop occasionally and look back. She may be telling you where her Romeo is. An adult doe traveling with one to three fawns, at any time, means she is not in heat, and there will probably not be a buck traveling behind them. More than one adult doe traveling together probably means a buck has started collecting his harem and he is probably close by. See if the does look back. They may tell you where the buck is.

➢ When a deer comes into shooting range, is it nervous? If yes, you've got less time to do whatever before it may spook and vanish. Is it in or will it enter your scent trail? If yes, it will probably do a quick exit and "blow" an alarm to all the deer population in the area. When this happens, you probably will not see a deer the rest of that hunting session. Keep a close look at the head. As long as its head is down, you can continue moving slowly into shooting position (if you are not already there). Is the deer browsing, moving fast, or running? If they are browsing, it means you've got more time to get into shooting position – move slowly. It also means you'll have a still or slow-moving target. If it is moving fast or running, say "B-a-a-a-a" as it enters a shooting lane. I'm not joking. It works almost every time, even if it is in a dead run. It will normally stop and look around to determine the source of your sound. You must already be in shooting position when you say "B-a-a-a-a". Some hunters whistle but "B-a-a-a-a" works best for me. Your volume should be just loud enough for the deer to hear you above its own noise, as it moves through the leaves. You should have a second or two to aim and fire before the deer decides to move on. If a deer, traveling in good cover, comes to an opening, like a logging road, it may stop for a moment before crossing to check for danger. This makes a dandy opportunity for a still shot.

➢ Quickly decide your target. Broad sided shots are best. Aim for a double lung shot (especially during archery season). This target is large and, if executed properly, the deer will not go very far (fifty to three hundred yards). When hunting near a bluff, where the deer could run after being shot, aim for the shoulder at mid-point, if using a gun or muzzleloader. Bone fragments will penetrate the lungs along with the bullet. This shot puts it on the ground immediately and gets the vitals too. Shoulder shots do destroy more meat than one just behind the shoulder. Some hunters aim at the point of its shoulder joint (heart shot). This target is low on the whitetail, so if you shoot a little low, you'll miss. Some aim for the neck. This target is small. Learn where the vital area (kill zone) is located. If necessary, use life size paper targets to practice with, until you aim for the kill zone instinctively. Note the kill zone on the target below. In the real world of hunting, you may not see a dream target. It may be standing behind a tree or some other obstruction. If you're using a gun, this may not be a serious problem. If you see a head, aim just below the base of the horns, if it has any. A hit here and the deer will drop like a rock. If you see a side view of the rear end, aim for the pelvic bone area. This will be between the base of its tail and about half forward of the ham and about four inches from topside. This shot will not kill a deer but you'll be able to run it down and finish it off. If the only thing that you see is the mid section, aim for the back bone, about three to four inches down from topside. This shot should drop it, but you'll need to finish it off with a shot to the neck. If it is going from you, where should you aim? During archery season, you should wait and hope that it turns broadside before it gets out of range or say "B-a-a-a-a" softly and hope it turns to investigate, rather than bolt and run. During gun season, pick the spine for a target (or butt if hunting on the ground). When shooting from a tree stand, aim a bit higher than if you were on the ground. Draw an imaginary line through its vitals back to you to determine your proper aim point.

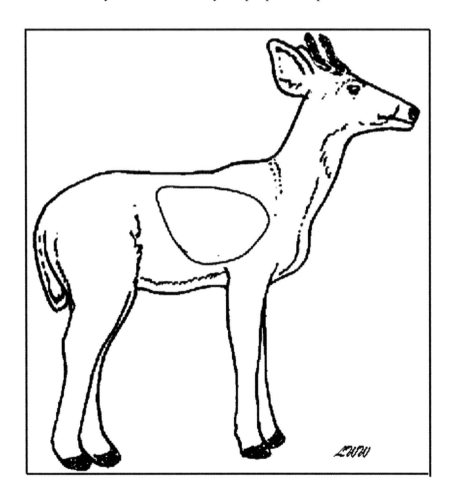

➤ Aim well and squeeze the trigger. Don't squeeze unless your sights are on target and you are positive that your target is a legal deer. I remember one rifle season at last light on a new stand that had high potential; I saw a big black body behind a cedar limb. I almost squeezed the trigger, until I realized, "that's a mighty big deer". It was a cow and I had hiked an hour to the very backside of a Wildlife Management Area to this stand. Make your first shot count. It's unlikely that you will get a second shot, while it is standing still. Brace your weapon on whatever you have available - tree trunk, gun rest if your tree stand is so equipped, or place your elbows on your knees. If you are standing/walking on the ground, ease down on one knee and brace your elbow on the other knee. Off handed shooting is OK at close range, but I'll use a rest then also if I can. Make sure your bullet/arrow will not hit a branch or twig.

➤ After you shoot - Did it run (if it did) with its tail up or down? It is VERY IMPORTANT to look at its tail after you shoot. Up means you missed and down means it's hit. Precisely what direction did it go (if it went anywhere at all)? Pick out trees, bushes, rocks, logs, etc. that you will recognize when you get to the spot. If you're using a bow, did you see fletching as it ran? If so, precisely where on the deer did you see it? Sit at your stand for a moment and calm down. Review exactly what you saw after you squeezed the trigger and burn it into memory. You will need accurate recall if it did not fall in sight of your stand. Did it run with tail up? Did you see blood on its side? Plan your next moves. If it's bow season, give the deer time to die if it is hit hard, but not enough time for it to lie down and let the blood coagulate if it is not hit hard. Personally, I use about fifteen minutes.

Chapter Eight
Other Hunting Methods

Ideally, hunters should use stand hunting as their primary hunting method and use still hunting, drive hunting, and boat hunting methods in the middle of the day or all day, on those days weather conditions render stand hunting ineffective, or when deer movement otherwise declines. There are occasions when still/drive/boat hunting are not only appropriate, but also will improve a hunter's overall performance in the woods. Once you master these methods, you should become a better hunter, than the average stand hunter.

❖ General - During the following weather conditions, still/drive/boat hunting may be more productive than stand hunting:
  ➢ Heavy rain - Once a front moves in, deer movement all but stops, and you would be better off still-hunting.
  ➢ Humid days - Deer tend to sit tight on humid days. Don't cancel a hunting trip because of the humidity level. Rather, consider still, drive, or boat hunting on these days.
  ➢ Cold low wind-chill days - Concentrate on the sunny sides of hills (even edges of pasture fields, that have a bit of cover), swamps, and dense evergreens. Wind chill can be twenty degrees Fahrenheit warmer in these places.
  ➢ Windy days - During moderate to strong winds (especially during the late season, when the wind chill is severe). Conifers (thick evergreen groves) can reduce wind velocity by over half. This could be a still or drive hunter's dream.

Don't still hunt or drive hunt in the immediate areas that you plan to stand hunt in the near future. Doing so would tend to reduce deer sightings while stand hunting, because it would make the deer become more nocturnal and push them to thick cover.

❖ Still Hunting - For simplicity, this book considers still and stalk hunting as the same hunting method. Both still and stalk hunting require the hunter to play like a ghost and sneak through the woods virtually unnoticed by the game. When still hunting, the hunter is looking for the game. When stalk hunting, the hunter knows about where the game is and "stalks" the game, trying to get close enough or, otherwise, find an opportunity to make a kill. Actually, a whitetail hunter using this ploy would likely switch back and forth between still and stalk hunting on most any hunt day. Some hunters are better still/stalk hunters than others. I've heard of hunters that could follow a deer around for hours, undetected by the deer. If you're this good at still hunting, then, by all means, you should use this method more than other hunters. It must take years of practice to become this proficient. Some people just cannot sit still, as is required for stand hunting. Still/drive/boat hunting are very appropriate for these people. Still hunting, as used in this book, is where the hunter moves slowly and quietly through the woods looking as deep into the woods ahead and to the sides as the eye can be trained to look. Still hunting basics are as follows:

Have a plan. Skirt the outside edges of heavy cover, up dry branches or swamps, spending more time at deer trails and points that protrude into open timber. Follow logging roads, stopping and watching at deer trails, another logging road intersecting, and anywhere the logging road cuts through heavy cover. Follow ridge tops, moving along one edge for about a hundred yards, sneaking across to the other side, and following that edge, etc. Still hunting is more difficult on flat terrain, because whitetail can more easily spot your movement. Don't forget to look behind you and to the sides occasionally. Don't walk over ridge tops; peek over

73

them, while staying close to cover. Don't let the deer silhouette you against the sky. Walk into the wind, or at least not with the wind, when possible to prevent deer ahead of you from smelling you and relocating before you ever get a quick glimpse of them. When you're forced to walk with the wind, walk fast. It's doubtful you will see a deer then anyway. Try to spend most of the time in more productive areas (primarily in/near bedding areas) with a good deer population. When in more productive areas, take two or three steps and stop for a minute or two, looking for movement, colors that don't belong, or deer body parts. By the time the still hunter sees a whole deer, it's probably got its tail up and running. By taking just a few steps, a deer in hearing distance may think its just another deer, or some other animal, and not spook and run before you see it. To a deer, continuous steps means predator. Some still hunters consider their hunting method, "mobile stand hunting", since they spend more time still/looking than moving. Some highly productive areas may merit sitting for an hour or more, especially during late evening. A good still hunter may not move two to four miles in a day.

Learn to walk while making minimum noise and movement. If the leaves are rather dry or the ground is frozen and each step makes a loud "crunch", strongly consider NOT using this hunting method, no matter how good you become. There's a skill to walking quietly and it is exhausting to execute properly. Slowly transfer weight from one foot to the other. Set your heel down first and slowly roll the rest of your foot down. Plan each step. Avoid twigs/sticks that may say, "snap", when your full body weight is across them. Avoid stepping on a rock that your body weight will shift and then it will say, "clunk", as it settles back against the rock under or next to it. Look for moss-covered areas, rock-outcroppings, sand, dry mud, etc. that will be quiet underfoot. As you walk, try to end each series of steps so you are standing by a tree or other cover. If you are hunting by a highway, move when there is a car passing. Take this advantage when planes fly over, etc. the same way. Wear soft-finish outer garments and soft-soled shoes to reduce noise. Watch for a passable general direction ahead of you that will minimize your moving and cracking branches. When you push branches out of your way, move them slowly. Be careful not to bend dead limbs very far or they will say, "crack". Don't lean against saplings or use them as hand holds. On a calm day it's like waving a flag. When crossing water, don't splash. Splashing water is an alarming sound to deer. When you make a noise, remain motionless for a few minutes. If a deer hears your noise, it may look in the direction of the noise for several minutes before continuing to browse. Cluck on a turkey call or sound a "buck bawl" to make deer think turkey or another deer makes your noises.
If you see a deer, freeze. If it is moving toward you, slowly begin getting into shooting position, when its head is behind trees, etc. If it is moving away from you, continue your slow movements in its direction. Now you're actually in the stalking mode.

If you are hunting in wide-open prairie/desert/plains type terrain, stop at high, good vantage point spots, and use binoculars to scan the low areas for movement. If you see a trophy that you are interested in, watch it until it beds down and begin easing toward it. During the last one to two hundred yards (depending on available cover) you may have to low crawl to get in range for your weapon. If you start moving toward the whitetail, while it is still moving, you will lose track of it, once you get to its elevation. Actually, this is a classical stalk hunting ploy.

While still hunting, look for potential new stand locations. This is an ideal way to scout new areas or to re-scout areas, looking for changes in travel patterns.

❖ Drive Hunting - Drive hunting requires a minimum of two hunters working together as a team. One hunter walks through/near a potential bedding/feeding area, allowing their scent to drift ahead/through the driven area, and hopefully causes a deer or two to move toward his buddy hunter(s). This method works best if you have hunting buddies that are not trigger-happy. Have a plan that each hunter understands for each drive. The stander(s) need to know roughly where to expect the driver to be exiting the driven area. The driver(s) may consider wearing head-to-toe hunter orange. A semi-automatic rifle or shotgun with buckshot (if legal in your area) works well when driving. Some good drivers say that they would rather drive than be a stander, because they've killed more deer driving than standing. Such hunters are probably good still hunters.

You must know where to drive. Walking by a thicket, allowing your scent to drift ahead of you and hopefully down through the thick growth, will cause the deer to relocate. Use your scent to drive rather than sound or visibility. Contrary to some beliefs, the driver should walk as quietly as possible. If a deer hears the driver, it will pinpoint exactly where he is. If the deer knows exactly where the driver is, they may "sit tight" and allow the driver to pass or walk around the driver. The driver must walk very slowly. Give the deer time to get nervous enough to run before you get to its position or it may let you pass. The driver should zigzag if driving a wide area. Zigzagging will make it more difficult for the deer to determine exactly where you are headed. The stander(s) should pick a spot where trails come out of the thick cover, and they have good visibility, preferably on some elevated spot, and remain ready to make a quick shot.

The biggest problem encountered when drive hunting is preventing the deer from "popping" out the sides of the driven area. It's more often the wise old buck and older does that tends to do this. To reduce this possibility, the driven area should be rather short, and be bordered by lakes, fields, or some other barrier to the deer. If you have several drivers, let one hang back from the rest in case the whitetails let the driver(s) pass and then makes a run for it. Deer handle one threat extremely well, but a second threat normally "blind-sides" them. If the terrain allows, and the driven area is narrow (like a large brier patch), place the stander(s) on high ground and walking about fifty yards ahead of the driver, moving at the same pace as the driver, rather than at the end of the driven area. This "twist" may allow the stander(s) to see a deer sneaking out the sides of the driven area.

There is another application of drive hunting that deserves a special note. Occasionally you will hunt a smart old buck that evades the stand hunting method, no matter where you set-up for him. Maybe he is very nocturnal, takes a different route each time he returns to his bedding, or who knows. But, you know where he beds and roughly how big he is. You've seen his tracks, scrapes, and/or rubs. Drive hunting may be the perfect method to use to get him out in the open, where you can get a shot at him.

❖ Boat Hunting - Whitetails seem to be drawn to water. It may be because the area offers an abundance of preferred foods. Sometimes it is because the area is too rough/remote for hunters to walk to. Also, large bodies of water sometimes moderate the temperature (cooler on hot days and warmer on cold days); thus, the deer may seek such areas of moderated temperatures. Using a boat to get to, otherwise, isolate areas can allow you to hunt virgin areas. This method can also involve floating or cruising the shores looking for bedded or browsing whitetail. This method is legal, but shooting a swimming deer from a boat, or elsewhere, is illegal in all states that I am aware, and certainly unsporting also. Most states disallow shooting from a boat if the engine is running.

Using a boat to get to islands and landlocked terrains can open a world of opportunity. Shorelines are often state property for some distance from the shore, making such locations legal hunting. When hunting pressure becomes severe, deer may swim to islands or move to the remote backwoods that may be accessible by boat. Islands, especially long narrow ones, are ideal areas for using drive hunting, because the water serves as a perfect natural barrier, preventing the deer from "popping out" the sides of the driven area. Remote areas that are accessible by boat may have more trophy bucks than heavily hunted, easy to get to areas. Such areas may be especially appropriate for hunters with moderate walking disabilities.

Cruising/floating the banks looking for a whitetail is another application of boat hunting. This method is similar to still hunting, but allows the hunter to cover much more territory and to do so quieter than using conventional still hunting. Deer do not seem to fear a human in a boat like they do a human in the woods. Perhaps this is because they see fishermen in boats routinely, posing no threat to them. Normally they simply stay still until you pass. When a deer does spook from the sight of a hunter in a boat, they may not run far before stopping. Train your eye to see a body part of a bedded deer or one standing still as you drift/cruise the banks. This is likely what you will see as you drift/cruise the waters edges. Sound simple? Don't count on it. Even at twenty yards and in full view, it's not easy to see a bedded or standing deer. Most people float past and never know the deer are in the world. Boat hunting normally takes you to the whitetail's bedding areas or perhaps areas they will browse for a midday snack. As hunting pressure increases and the whitetails search out secluded areas, this becomes truer. This means that boat hunting can be more productive at mid day than at dawn or dusk. Therefore, consider using boat hunting as a fill-in between the morning and evening stand hunts. If you just can't stand the idea of getting out of bed to go hunting at some strange predawn hour, maybe this hunting method would be perfect for you.

What boat should you use when cruising/floating the shorelines looking for whitetail? The answer may depend on the type of river that you intend to float. Some hunters prefer a canoe, but you better be experienced with a canoe if this is your choice. A bass boat may work if you've got adequate water depth to float it. Personally, I vote for a duck/goose hunting type boat. They are normally an aluminum construction with a twenty-five to sixty horsepower engine and they will float in rather shallow water. This allows the hunter to maneuver shallow water to stay close to the banks.

Chapter Nine
Hunting the Trophy Bucks

Trophy hunting is great, but there's nothing wrong with meat hunting if you use legal methods. In fact, many states are beginning to encourage "antlerless" kills by limiting the number of whitetail harvested with antlers over three inches long. The objective of such laws is to allow the small bucks to live longer and develop a mature rack and, in some cases, to control the whitetail populations by harvesting more does. For years I halfheartedly hunted for the trophies, but during archery or muzzleloader season I was determined to put at least one legal deer in the freezer, trophy or not. After I became a more skillful whitetail hunter and the whitetail herds grew to healthy numbers, my primary objective became hunting for a trophy.

Realize that the definition of a trophy varies from hunter to hunter and from area to area. If I had never killed anything larger than a spike, a four-point kill may be a trophy to me. Also, taking a four-point with a bow is just as admirable trophy, to me, as taking a ten-point with a muzzleloader, 30-30 pistol, shotgun, or rifle. I remember one archery season I missed two eight or ten point bucks, and saw three more equals that would have been easy targets with most any gun. Those of you who have not hunted trophies with a bow may say: "Man, you need to learn to shoot". Well, trophy bucks do not walk out into an opening, stay in one spot, or come within thirty yards of your tree like a doe, fawn, or spike will. An easy trophy shot with a bow is rare! It seems that trophy bucks normally force the hunter to shoot through little holes, dodge limbs, or something. Also a Boone and Crocket score (discussed later in this chapter) of 125 taken in Florida or South Georgia may be more of a trophy to a hunter than one with a score of 170 taken in northern Michigan. Some areas just have bigger deer/racks than others. If a whitetail hunter cannot afford to travel to the nation's pockets of big deer/racks, an admirable goal would be to harvest a buck with the best Boone and Crocket score for the area that they hunt.

If you decide to trophy buck hunt, scout during the spring looking for trophy antler sheds. This tells you that he's still alive, his rack size, and where you may find him next fall. Concentrate on scrape areas in or around heavy cover (See Chapter Five under "Funnel Them to You – Hunt near scrapes). Learn to use deer calls (See Chapter Seven under "Talking to Trophy Bucks"). Learn to pick a stand to control your scent trail (See Chapter Five under Controlling Your Scent Trail"). Use a portable tree stand when possible (See Chapter Five under "Picking Tree for Portable Tree Stand" and Chapter Twelve under "Portable Tree Stand"). Don't ever shoot an adult doe traveling alone or one of several adult does traveling together. The buck is probably not far behind. This is a VERY IMPORTANT point if you are serious about hunting for trophy bucks. Don't shoot less than trophy bucks. In a year or two he may be a trophy buck. Also, you are not going to kill a trophy after your kill tags are filled with less than trophy bucks. Be at your stand at early dawn and last light and consider spending the entire day at your stand on days that the weather and/or the stand's potential justify doing so. Concentrate on learning to see and recognize deer body parts. Concentrate on shady areas rather than areas with full light. Trophy bucks (and old does) are more secretive, less curious, more nocturnal, and harder to see than younger deer. When you are on your stand, scan cover for unnatural lines. Look for curved horizontal lines of a back, sapling trunks that could be legs, wet/black noses, antler tips, ear tips, etc. Once located, watch intently for movement. If you think you saw a deer, you probably did and it probably was a buck. If you think you see a deer body part, turn your scope power up and look at it through your scope (don't forget to turn it back down). Stay at your evening stand until the last second of shooting light. The largest racks that I've ever seen in the woods were right at dark.

Some trophy bucks have survived by hiding under our noses. For example, subdivisions with a few vacant and grown up lots may be all the cover required to make a trophy buck feel at home (See Chapter Three under "Private Property - Residential or industrial areas for archery season"). Call Wildlife Resources Agencies to find out which counties or WMA's have the best trophy records. Since age is one of the variables determining rack size, look for WMA's that have been closed for a year or two, limit kills to trophies only, or have very short hunting seasons. Look for private lands that have been posted for years and had very little hunting pressure. Sometimes, areas with very poor deer population will produce a few good wall hangers. Most hunters will not hunt an area with a poor deer population; therefore, bucks in these areas will likely live longer. They will probably have more foods and minerals to pick from. You may hunt for days before seeing a deer in areas like this, but when you see one, it may be a wall hanger. If you think your hunting area has mature bucks with good genetics, put out deer salt and deer blocks specifically formulated to develop trophy racks (See Chapter One under "Whitetail's Vulnerabilities - Food and Sex" and then under "Food").

Based on personal experience and state statistics, following are a few states that should have heavier than average rack development: Idaho, Illinois, Indiana, Iowa, Kentucky, Louisiana, Maine, Maryland, Michigan, Minnesota, Mississippi, Missouri, Nevada, New Jersey, Oklahoma, Pennsylvania, South Dakota, Texas, Virginia, Wisconsin, and West Virginia. See the Appendix for more details.

If you decide to trophy buck hunt, this book will certainly fulfill your need, but you must take its content much more seriously than the average reader. Read it several times. I assure you that you will get more and more from this book the more that you learn about deer hunting. If you decide you want to harvest a deer, you can hunt almost anywhere as long as you have permission. But, if you want to harvest a trophy whitetail buck, research as much as possible. You may be lucky enough to live in an area where trophy deer are regularly harvested. If you live in such an area, then there are probably relative's/friend's land on which you can hunt or maybe even a WMA. But, there are so many luck hunters in the WMA's; they'll likely get him before you do. I remember hunting a small WMA for a specific deer once. When I walked out of the woods for lunch, on opening day of the first muzzleloader hunt, there he was. My trophy was dead and shot by a luck hunter. The hunter said he got cold at 8:30 AM and went back to the vehicle for coffee (It was only forty-five degrees that morning). When he went back, he went to sleep in a shallow ditch and woke up when a deer jumped over him. He rose up and shot. Is this a classic or what?

The most productive time to harvest a trophy whitetail is undoubtedly during the rut. Half the battle is getting to know your quarry (where he sleeps, eats, and travels). If you hear of a trophy buck being seen, find out exactly where he was seen, which direction he was headed, and what time of day he was seen. This information will tell you whether the buck was moving toward or away from his bedding area. Then find out as much about him as you can by scouting that area. Spend every available moment studying what you have learned about him.

The variables affecting a buck's rack size are food and minerals in their diet, genetics, buck to doe ratio, and the buck's age. A buck does not reach maturity until he is three years old. During his first three years, body development takes priority over antler growth. Three through five years of age is a buck's prime. Generally a buck will start to decline after that. Some bucks will still have antlers fairly close to prime until they reach the age of seven. Available nutrition/food will determine how long a buck remains in his prime.

Food and nutrition impacts a buck's antler development. The organic makeup of antlers during their development is almost all protein. Even after hardening is complete, a significant amount of protein remains in these antlers. The most important factor in growing trophy antlers is to provide the buck with nutrient rich foods during the antler development period from April through October. To grow the best set of antlers that his genetics and age will allow, a deer needs food containing at least sixteen percent digestible crude protein. Bucks also need digestible calcium during and after the antler growth period. A buck can borrow calcium from his skeleton and utilize it for antler growth, but he still needs foods that contain a minimum of a half of one percent calcium. Vitamin D is important in promoting calcium absorption and mineralizing the bone. A buck gets all the Vitamin D he needs by absorbing ultraviolet light through his skin and eating vegetation that has been in direct sunlight. It is believed that a buck needs a minimum of three tenths of one percent phosphorus in his diet for normal antler growth and other body needs. Vitamin A is important to antler development once the bone hardening begins. Carotenes in green leaves can be converted to Vitamin A. Green leaves are an important part of the deer's diet, even during the winter months, when green growth is scarce.

The buck to doe ratio of a deer herd impacts bucks' antler development. A buck to doe ratio of 1:1 to 1:3 is good. If a deer herd reaches a buck to doe ratio of 1:5 or more, there is heavy hunting pressure on bucks and most bucks will probably be under the age of three. There are some areas where the average age of bucks harvested may be one and one-half years of age. There will not be any Boon and Crockett records (discussed below) come out of deer herds like this. This problem can be corrected by harvesting only antlerless deer and trophy bucks. Now, would hunters have to measure the beams/tines and calculate a Boon and Crockett score before shooting a legal trophy buck? No, because this is not realistic. But point limits could logically be set for legal kills. Some states are using this system in selected WMA's. This system will cause the buck to doe ratio to become more favorable for antler development and create more rutting activity. The fittest bucks do most of the doe breeding.

Genetics impact bucks' antler development. The deer and antler size generally increases as you move further north within the United States. Well, we may argue that it's not a genetic difference but a temperature difference. Northern deer have to put on fat to survive the tough winters and this nutrition may create big bodies as well as the big racks. But, then, why do you find some monster body/rack bucks in south Georgia, where most buck deer look like jack rabbits with a wad of grass on their head? What about those whoppers in Virginia, Texas, Missouri, etc.? It's genetics. A hunter in South Georgia once told me that there are twenty-one subspecies of the whitetail. Well, I didn't believe him, but maybe there's some hint of truth to his statement? I'm sure that there are ways of genetically engineering monster bucks by means of DNA engineering via artificial insemination, but are we hunters willing to fund this expensive type of deer herd management?

Trophies that qualify for Boone and Crockett listings can be taken by several means, including rifle, muzzleloader, and archery equipment. In fact, even antlers found on the ground can be listed, although they are not eligible for some of the awards. More specialized trophy competitions have been organized for archery hunters and muzzleloader hunters, although they use the same measuring system as Boone and Crockett. The archery records are kept by an organization called Pope and Young. The Longhunter Society keeps the muzzleloader records. An archer or muzzleloader hunter could have a trophy listed in both Boone and Crockett and one of the specialized listings. There are several ways of scoring a whitetail's rack; but the most widely recognized and used is the Boone and Crocket method. Boone and Crockett recognizes two rack types: typical and non-typical (sometimes called atypical). A typical rack is rather symmetrical and a non-typical or atypical is all other shapes. The minimum scores to be recognized by Boon and Crockett for the record book are: 170 for Typical and 195 for non-typical. The minimum scores to be recognized by Pope and Young for the archery record book are: 125 for typical and 155 for non-typical. The largest trophy that I've killed was a typical and it scored about 110 using Boone and Crockett scoring rules. By most hunter's standards, it is a very nice rack. However, the record score is about 304 and "found deads" reach 333. This should give you an idea of how racks vary. The Boon and Crockett scoring rules deal with (1) the inside spread, in inches, taken perpendicular to the axis of the head at the widest point between the main beams, (2) the outside length of each main beam, (3) the length of each regular point and its corresponding point on the other main beam, (4) the circumference of the antler at the smallest point between the burr and the first point and, finally, (5) subtracts the length of all irregular points that measure one inch or greater. You can find more detailed information and official scoring sheets at http://www.boone-crockett.org/.

Chapter Ten
After You Shoot

Once you squeeze the trigger the fun is over and the work begins. The deer should be near where you shot but a buck, pumped full of adrenalin, may go several hundred yards with a hole in its heart. If it's not nearby it's your duty, as a hunter, to hunt for it!

❖ Tracking Wounded Deer - Locate precisely where the deer was when you shot, using the mental picture that you burned into memory immediately after you shot. There should be major turned-up leaves and earth, where it bolted after you shot. There probably will be cut hair and some blood if there were an exit hole. Look at the hair and try to determine the body part that you hit. Tie a surveyor's ribbon or something there. This will become your primary reference point, during your search for the deer, if it is not lying near by. If you do not find blood or hair, look for skinned limbs/saplings or a plowed trench where your bullet hit. If it's bow season, look for your arrow. Once found, inspect the arrow. Red blood on the arrow means artery blood, dark blood means vein blood, blood bubbles and/or white chunks means lung shot, and just hair and tallow probably means superficial wound.

Now, go to the point that you last saw the deer, looking for blood drops on the ground and/or foliage as you go. Tie surveyor's ribbons or something at these spots. It may take a few yards before it started bleeding well. If the bullet/arrow went through, it will start bleeding sooner, assuming that you shot from a tree stand. The body cavity must fill to the lowest hole, before it starts bleeding well. The lower the hit in the cavity, the sooner it will start bleeding. Whether the deer is traveling uphill or down hill also impacts cavity blood "leaking" from the lowest hole; therefore, impacting the blood trail.

Track the blood trail (if you do not see the deer lying near-by). You may not find blood but every several yards. In this case hang surveyor's ribbon, clothing, toilet paper, or whatever you have, on bushes at these spots. Tracking blood is easy in leaves, not too bad in green grass but is very difficult in pine needles, dry sage-grass, etc. If it's raining, even a drizzle, you better track fast. It doesn't take much rain to wash away the small blood spots. Don't let an inexperienced hunter go ahead of you, destroying the blood sign. Watch for blood on sapling trunks and bushes also. When the deer begins to get weak it will stagger against things. If you lose the blood trail, look back at your ribbons, clothing, toilet paper, etc. and determine the general direction the deer is headed and continue looking for blood in that direction. Look for tracks that it beat into the leaves, needles, ground, etc. Look for natural trails, that it could have used, and follow each one a ways looking for blood. Slowly walk semicircles past your last blood drop found. Ask yourself if there's a fence, gully, etc. ahead. Jumping such obstacles may drain their last ounce of energy. You may find it in or just beyond such obstacles. Ask yourself where it could be headed and check out the most probable for your circumstances. When wounded it may, continue in the same general direction, take the path of least resistance, use existing trails or a logging road, go down hill, go to water if handy, seek cover in ditches, brush, etc., or go toward home (bedding area). Home probably will be some thicket and may be miles from primary feeding.

I've tracked deer for over four hours before finding them. I had one circle back over the same trail that I had already tracked. This is tough tracking. Now you have to distinguish between

81

new blood and not so new blood. You can learn a lot about your hunting area by tracking a wounded deer. They will show you areas that you did not know existed!

How much time do you have after the deer dies and is not field dressed, before the meat goes bad? The answer varies a lot. Temperature is the biggest variable. The quicker the deer gets field dressed, the better the meat will be. I shot one once at last light in cool temperatures, and it jumped over a bluff and lodged half way down. I was hunting by myself and had no rope in my vehicle, so I decided to leave it until morning. The meat was eatable but tasted different. A couple of other last light kills in warmer temperatures, where I could not pick up a blood trail, I waited until the next morning, found them, and the meat was fine.

❖ After You Find Your Deer - Field Dress (Remove intestines, stomach, liver, and heart)

Make sure the deer is dead. If it is not dead, finish it off with a neck shot just below the head or it may hurt you. Consider dragging the deer out of the area that you shot it, before you field dress it, if you plan to hunt on the spot in the near future. You may want to remove your coat, roll up your sleeves, and put your watch in your pocket. This is a gory job. Some hunters carry latex gloves for this part of deer hunting. Bleeding the deer is normally accomplished quite well by the damage caused by the bullet or arrow. If you make a headshot I recommend bleeding the deer by cutting its throat down to the juggler vein.

Remove the internals. The sooner the internals are removed, the sooner the body will cool, and the better the meat will be.

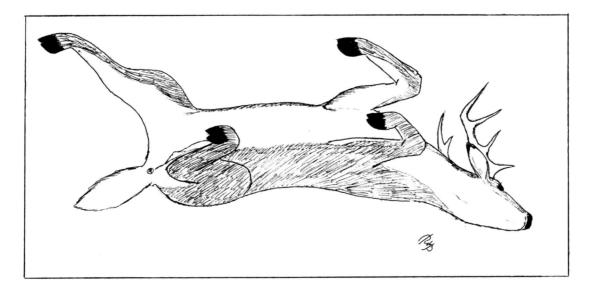

Turn the deer so it is belly up, as shown in the picture above. The objective is to remove the insides without cutting a gut, the stomach, or yourself. Some hunters carry fancy knives to do this, and may use them once or twice a year (or once in 2.2 years). Personally, I use a normal (but sharp) pocketknife. Make a very shallow incision with the point of the knife at the belly end of the sternum (brisket bone). DO NOT puncture the stomach or a gut. Forcefully hold your thumb about one-fourth inch up from the point, and on the side of the blade, as you make this incision, to avoid accidentally penetrating further than intended. Insert the knifepoint into the shallow incision, and make it long enough for you to place two fingers. Place two fingers into the incision, separating the muscles from the intestines, as shown in the picture below. Place the knife blade between your two fingers. Cut the hide and muscle as you move your two fingers toward the rear end, making sure that the blade point does not go under your finger (avoid cutting an intestine). Your incision should be ten to fourteen inches long, depending on the size of the deer. It should be no longer than necessary to get the intestines, stomach, liver, and heart out of the cavity, because when dragging the deer to the vehicle, the longer the incision the more likely it is that leaves, dirt, etc. will get inside of the cavity and damage eatable meat.

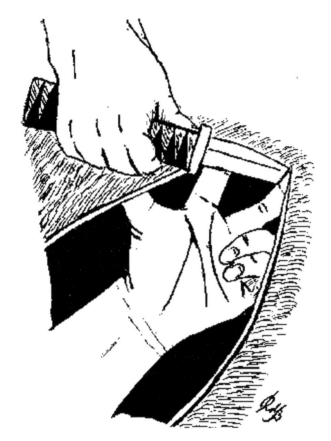

Reach into the cavity and bring the intestines out. Find the end going to its anus. Place your thumb and index finger on this gut, as close to its anus as you can easily reach. Strip the carne, inside, back a few inches and cut the gut. This will avoid carne getting on the meat. Reach into the cavity and begin cutting the diaphragm from around the ribcage. Reach into its cavity and remove the stomach, liver, heart, and lungs, cutting whatever hangs as you pull them out. Don't forget to cut the stomach open and see what it has been eating and try to determine where it had traveled to get it.

Dispose of the entrails. Some hunters leave them lying wherever and hunt on the same spot the next day. I feel that this creates an unnatural odor, so I try to get them out of the area, if I plan to hunt there during next few days. Also, I don't like the idea of other hunters finding my "gut piles". I try to hide them; otherwise, I may have company when I return to hunt the spot. At this point, you'll probably want to clean your hands (if you did not wear latex gloves). If there is a stream nearby, the solution is simple. If there is not water handy, use leaves to get the worst off. Moss or even dirt can be used to scrub the last off.

Don't forget to tie your kill tag to the deer. Game wardens frown on us coming out of the deer woods, dragging a deer and it not tagged. I carry plastic ties in my wallet, during deer season, for this purpose. Cut a hole in an ear, or some other body part, or tie it around the base of the antlers.

❖ Transport the deer - Some people buy a fancy wheelbarrow/dolly to roll them out. I seldom hunt in terrain that I could push or pull a wheelbarrow. Some hunters carry a "pull rope" that may not get used but once or twice per year. I use my tree stand's safety belt. I put one loop around my waist and lace it tight. I kneel down and put the other loop around the deer's head or antlers. When I stand up, the deer's head is off the ground a few inches and will not hang on logs/brush as I move toward my vehicle. Now hopefully it's all down hill to the vehicle (I wish).

Don't strap the deer carcass to the hood of your vehicle. It may be macho but the engine heat sure doesn't help the meat. A nice rack can be rough on the vehicle hood's paint job also. Blood draining onto the vehicle paint can damage the paint also. Even if you transport the deer in a pickup truck bed, you should wash the blood from any painted surfaces, after unloading the deer, to avoid paint damage.

Now that the deer is field dressed, how much time do I have before the deer must be skinned, quartered, and refrigerated? The faster the hide comes off the faster it cools and the faster it cools the better the meat will be. If the temperature is above forty-five degrees Fahrenheit, you need to be heading home or to the butcher. Stuffing the cavity full of bagged ice will make it cool faster. I've seen hunters ride around showing off their kill for two days. This is not smart.

Check it in at your closest check-in (checking) station. This will be a country store, filling station, hardware, etc. or may be WMA camp if it is a quota/managed hunt. Sometimes game biologists will be there to pull jawbones, etc. for the state's data bank.

Deer slaughter house or butcher it yourself? This is a personal decision and either alternative is fine. Where is the deer slaughterhouse? Ask someone at the check-in station who butchers deer in the area. You must leave the permanent kill tag with the deer in this case. Butcher it yourself? See Chapter Eleven for step-by-step instructions.

Chapter Eleven
Butchering Your Deer

There's nothing wrong with hiring a butcher to process your whitetail kill. I always preferred to butcher it myself. I learned by trial and error on my own, so it must not be too difficult - especially since you've got the following directions.

❖ Butchering Chart

Butcher Chart

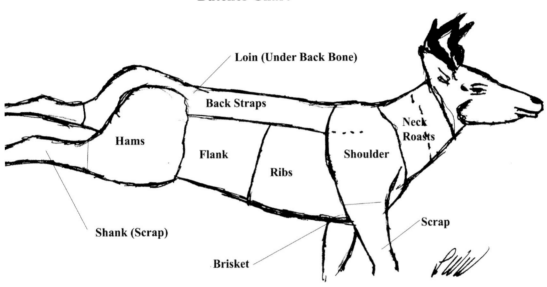

❖ Skin and Quarter
  ➢ Hang it on a tree limb, a garage or barn ceiling joist, etc. by its back legs. Cut a hole where the two layers of skin meet each other at the shank. Insert/tie two ropes (or light duty tie-down straps) to the deer using these holes. Hoist it up until its head is just off the floor/ground. The back legs should be apart.
  ➢ Cut around both legs at the top of the shank. Cut from these cuts, along the top of the rump, to the bottom of its anus. Cut/saw through the anus, continuing through the tailbone. You'll need a hacksaw or reciprocating saw. Pull the hide away from the hams and down over its body, cutting between the hide and the body as required. When you get to the shoulders, cut the hide around the legs at the end of the large part of the shoulder. Cut/saw the front legs off at this cut and discard. Cut the hide along the top of the shoulders, ending at its brisket (center of chest). Peel the hide off the shoulders. Cut the hide completely from top down to the brisket incision. Continue pulling the hide down over its shoulders and on down, as far as you can, on its neck. The neck area is rough going. You'll have to make several between the hide and neck cuts. Cut/saw the head off, as close to the hide as possible, and discard the hide and head (or save it for the taxidermist if you're going to mount the head or have the hide tanned).
  ➢ Remove the shoulders - Pull the shoulders away from the ribs and cut the meat between them.
  ➢ Remove the neck roast - Depending on the size of the deer, you may want to make one or two cuts. If it is a large or medium deer, cut/saw halfway between the neck stub and

where the shoulders were attached. Make a second cut/saw at the point the shoulders were attached. If it is a small deer, cut/saw at the point the shoulders were attached.

➤ Remove ribs/flank - Saw on both sides of the brisket bone, so the ribs will no longer be attached to it, and discard the brisket. Cut/saw the flank and ribs halfway between the rib stubs and where the "back strap" meat starts on both sides. Cut/saw the flank and ribs, next to where the "back strap" meat starts, on both sides.

➤ Remove loin (Located inside the ribs near the back bone and toward the pelvic cavity) - Starting just below the pelvic cavity, pull/cut the two meaty muscles from inside next to its backbone. Stay out of the inside of pelvic cavity, to avoid puncturing its bladder.

➤ Remove the two "back straps" (T-bone steak of a deer, without the bone). Starting just below the hams, cut in from two directions (the ribs and to the side of the backbone) removing the meat. Keep your knife as close to the bone as possible. Continue cutting all the way down the back, ending where you removed the neck roast. Remove the second "back strap" the same way. An alternative would be to saw across the backbone for chops but why store all that bone and waste freezer space.

➤ Remove hams - Cut/saw one leg (shank) from the ham, just above the large part of the ham. Cut along the pelvic bone, starting at the anus end of the ham. Remove the ball from the socket and then tear/cut the remainder of the ham from the pelvic bone. The weight of the ham will help tear if off (be careful not to drop the ham). While still hanging, remove the second ham from the pelvic bone as outlined above and discard the backbone and pelvic scrap. Cut/saw the second leg (shank) from the ham just above the large part of the ham.

➤ Chill the meat in a refrigerator set at forty or forty-five degrees Fahrenheit, for five to seven days, before further processing. This ageing makes the meat more tender.

❖ Prepare Venison For Freezer - This section will have limited detail, because there are so many directions to go at this point, and everyone prefers their own cuts of meat. I will simply try to give you your different alternatives, by cut, from the "Skin and Quarter" section above.

➤ Loin (The filet mignon of a deer) - This is a very tender all meat cut, and most people I know simply slice it cross the grain for breakfast frying meat. You could grind it into deer burger or make jerky but what a waste.

➤ Back straps - The same as loin above. It is almost as tender as the loin and tastes similar.

➤ Hams - If it is a small deer you could baste it in meat spices and grill it whole in a convection type grill. For a small or large deer you could remove each muscle, remove the tough white tendon material, surrounding each muscle, and cut it cross the grain for breakfast frying or steaks. Some people chill the meat and then saw the whole ham into steak slices. In this case the tough white tendon material, surrounding each muscle, ends up in each slice. Butchers normally take this approach, because it is faster. Other alternatives would be: Cut it in strips for jerky, grind it into deer burger, cut into sections for roasts (you could also baste these in meat spices and grill on a convection type grill), and cut into chunks for stew meat.

➤ Shoulders (They have more tendons than the hams) - I prefer making one or two roasts out of each shoulder (you could also baste these in meat spices and grill on a convection type grill). You can also grind the meat into deer burger, cut it in strips for jerky or cut into chunks for stew meat.

➤ Neck - Some people throw it away but it's good as a roast, stew meat, ground into deer burger, or cut into strips for jerky.

➤ Ribs - Some people throw them away also, but they are delicious boiled and then basted in meat spices and grilled. They can also be used like a stew meat or spare ribs.

Chapter Twelve
Equipment

Remember the analogy in Chapter One comparing the Allies liberating Kuwait to whitetail hunting? In addition to knowing Iraq's vulnerabilities and defenses and formulating a strategy to take advantage of both, the Allies had good equipment. Without having the state-of–the-art fighters, bombers, tanks, sighting systems, etc., it's doubtful that the Allies would have won the war in just a few days and with few casualties. Again, whitetail hunting is no different. The objective of this chapter is to provide you with a guide for selecting your hunting equipment. Trial and error in this area is expensive and detrimentally impacts your effectiveness as a whitetail hunter.

Disclaimer statement - The author of this book is not endorsing any particular brand of hunting equipment to the reader. No manufacturer or outfitter has paid the author for any form of advertising. The manufacturing brands, mentioned in this chapter and Chapter Thirteen, simply happen to be ones that the author has personal experience and success with and are mentioned to help hunters learn what is available on the market that performs well. The author of this book makes no warranty, either expressed or implied, concerning the performance, reliability, safety, or suitability of mentioned brands.

❖ Compound Bow/Crossbow - The anticipation that magnifies inside you, as the whitetail moves into range, is what whitetail hunting is all about. Will it come close enough for a shot, or will it vanish into the shadows like a ghost? Every minute seems like an hour as each new experience unfolds. If hunters carrying a rifle or a shotgun break sweat waiting for the exciting moment, imagine what it's like for the bow hunter. A rifle will bring down a deer at over a hundred yards. But the bow hunter has to hold his breath until the whitetail gets to within twenty to thirty yards. It just doesn't get any more exciting than that. I've bow hunted for the whitetail for the last thirty years, and this is the reason why. Additionally, bow hunting teaches the hunter things a gun hunter may never learn. Since a bow hunter must be able to get the whitetail within twenty or thirty yards for an effective shot, it teaches a hunter to select a stand that funnels the whitetail in close. Bow hunting forces a hunter to master scent trail control. It also teaches a hunter to remain calm, while a trophy buck moves closer, and anxiety tends to impair the hunter's reasoning ability.

Flat trajectory - To a bow/crossbow hunter, the bow/crossbow is the most important piece of equipment they carry to the woods. A compound bow or crossbow is very accurate and lethal, if you use good equipment, know its limitations, and practice. Don't try to use the old recurve or longbow antiques, unless you are willing to practice fanatically. They don't shoot the arrow; they "lob" it to the target. The trajectory is so horrible you must be able to judge distance to within a few feet to develop any degree of repeatability/accuracy. This is really tough when you're twenty feet up a tree that is on a steep slope. Unless you are really good with these bows, you'll wound and lose too many deer, and we should respect the whitetail enough not to subject them to this torture! There are a few hunters that can use these bows effectively. A compound bow or crossbow, for hunting the whitetail, should shoot close to a flat trajectory up to, at least, twenty-five yards. A hunter can use the same sight pin, and aim "dead center" of the kill zone, for all shots up to the limit of near flat trajectory. Accomplishing a near flat trajectory avoids guessing at yardage on shots up to this point. The first prerequisite to accomplishing an acceptably near flat trajectory is to pick a good compound bow or crossbow, and there are a lot of good ones available these days. I have personal experience with Hoyt and High Country. Other brands are Ben Pearson, Browning, Buckmaster, Champion, Chek-mate, Darton, Diamond, Fred Bear, Forge, Golden Eagle, Infinet, Jennings, Martin, Matthews, McPherson, Oneidaeagle, PSE, Reflex, and Trisectra. Crossbow brands, that I am familiar with, are Barnett and Horton. The second prerequisite to accomplishing an acceptably near flat trajectory is to set the bow draw weight as high as you can comfortably pull and hold. If this is less than sixty pounds you need to consider getting a legal permit to carry a crossbow. Crossbow draw weight is preset at the factory. The third prerequisite to accomplishing an acceptably near flat trajectory is to minimize the arrow and broad head combined weight. Shooting an arrow unnecessarily heavy will reduce your flat trajectory distance unnecessarily. Shooting an arrow that is too light for your bow, can result in splintered tines, similar to "dry firing" the bow. Shooting an arrow that is too limber will cause the arrow to flex unacceptably. However, using a bow equipped with overdraw (arrow rest closer to the string), reduces the required arrow length, which reduces arrow flex as well as arrow weight. Some hunters say use a heavy arrow to ensure that the arrow goes through the deer. Arrow penetration is important. If the broad head does not exit, the deer may not leave a good blood trail. However, I have not experienced problems with the broad head not exiting, using minimum weight arrows, unless the arrow hits serious bone. It's not uncommon for the arrow shaft to remain in the deer. This seems to make the deer bleed better than if the entire arrow goes through. Use carbon or aluminum arrows? An arrow MUST be straight to fly straight, and an aluminum arrow bends much more easily than carbon. Some hunters say use carbon arrows because they are lighter, but I've accomplished minimum arrow weight for my bow, using aluminum arrows. The optimum weight arrow in carbon or aluminum can be a good choice. The fourth prerequisite to accomplishing near flat trajectory is to maximize arrow speed. Try to accomplish an arrow speed approaching three hundred feet per second. This prerequisite, for the most part, is determined by the other three prerequisites.

Use a good string release. Finger release gives a slightly different side pressure each time you shoot unless you practice fanatically. A good release trigger will release the string precisely the same every time you shoot.

Crossbows are legal to use in most states if the hunter has a disability, disallowing the proper use of a bow. This does not mean you have to have one arm missing to qualify. If you have significant wrist, elbow, shoulder and/or back problems you may qualify. Call your state's Wildlife Management Agency for specific laws for your state.

Picking sights - Pick fluorescent or fiber-optic sights for your compound bow. In the woods, especially on a cloudy day or near dawn or dark, it's difficult to see your sights and the target at the same time. Fiber-optic sights are a more recent development. They are small cylinders, made under pressure, aligning the molecular chains with the filaments causing any absorbed light to run along the fiber's length and out the ends, creating a highly visible aiming point, even in poor light. They should be more effective and durable than the old fluorescent plastics. If you use a compound bow, choose sights and sight bracket that are a cast metal, not a thin sheet metal. When you let your bow down out of a tree stand, sights hang on limbs, may hit the ground rather hard, etc., and force is applied to the bracket that misaligns the sights if the bracket is not quite rigid. Use a string peep on your compound bow with a large hole to give you more light. Small peepholes are fine for competition, when you have plenty of time and light, but I sure don't recommend them in the woods. If you are legal to shoot a crossbow, use a good scope. It is just as important as the crossbow that it is sitting on. A good scope will not fog on the inside, will give more shooting time at dawn or near dark and is less likely for an optic to move and you see nothing when you start to sight in on a trophy.

Sight-in - Use exactly the same arrow you will be hunting with - broad head and all. An arrow just does not fly exactly the same with a field-tip, as with a broad head of the same weight. Use a dense rubber target. Other types either will not stop your arrow or you will not be able to pull the arrow/broad-head from the target. Take your first shots at ten yards and roughly adjust the pin. Take your next shots at twenty yards and readjust your sight pin rather accurately. Take your next shots at twenty-five yards. Are you still on target? Keep backing up five yards until your arrow begins to hit below the bulls-eye. This distance should be no less than twenty-five yards to be really effective in the woods. Once you've determined this maximum limit of your flat trajectory, fine-tune your sight pin. You may want to sight-in about two inches high. If you shoot for a double lung shot, two inches high will be effective. If your shot is a few yards over your first pin's limit, a couple inches low will also be effective. Once bow season opens, don't forget to tie surveyor ribbon at this distance around your tree to eliminate the need for guessing at distance within your flat trajectory range. Step on back to, say, forty yards. Get an idea of how much the arrow drops from the point you determined to be your flat trajectory limit. This will give you a good idea how much to raise your pin (or crosshairs) on the deer if it's, say, ten yards past your surveyor ribbons.

❖ Gun - The gun and its sighting device is the most important piece of equipment the gun hunter carries to the woods. Learning your gun(s) and how to safely and accurately use it (them) is important, but is only a small part of learning how to hunt the whitetail deer. A lot of whitetail hunters, that I know, spend more time and money on guns than they do learning the whitetail and how to hunt. Guns are infatuating to some people and entertaining to shoot and that is OK; but don't be guilty of thinking that the gun and its sighting device is all there is to hunting the whitetail. Hunting the whitetail just isn't that simple.

Select the appropriate gun for the job. There are a lot of good guns on the market today. It doesn't take an expensive gun to do the job. Most of the guns that I use were preowned. It doesn't take a cannon to kill a deer. Most state laws require that we use a 0.24 caliber (5.9 mm) or larger. The longest shot in the woods that I've had to make was one hundred and thirty yards. I accomplished this shot with a muzzleloader. About the only time you would have an opportunity at longer distances is if you were road hunting (and this is illegal/unsporting) or hunting in some part of the country having minimal cover. Realize that the more the energy (knockdown power) a gun has, the more the gun may kick and the heavier the gun may be to carry; therefore, it behooves the hunter to get enough gun to do the job and no more. For every action, there is an equal and opposite reaction (to some degree).

I use the following guns for deer hunting:

➢ Ruger Model M77 Mark II, 7mm Rem. Magnum, bolt action with a Leupold 3x-9x-variablex40 scope. I carry this gun most of the time during gun season, especially if I'm hunting next to a bluff, where I could lose the deer if it were to travel a couple hundred yards after I hit it. I use one hundred and sixty-five grain, Sierra Gameking BTSP Federal premium shells which have a velocity of 2800 feet per second and energy of 2865 foot-pound at one hundred yards. It's rather light and has a composition, shock absorbing

89

stock. When I bang it on my tree stand, it doesn't skin it like it would if I used a beautiful walnut stock gun.

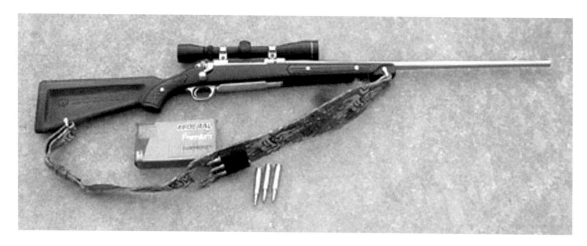

➢ Browning Bar 243 semi-automatic with a Redfield 3x-9x-variablex40 scope. I carry this gun when I'm planning to do some driving or still-hunting where two or three shots in quick succession may be required, and use ninety-five grain, CXP2, high velocity, ballistic silver tip, Winchester Supreme shells. This gun is light and has very little recoil, allowing me to hold on target, as I shoot more than one shot. Some hunters feel the 243 doesn't have enough knockdown power, but I've not experienced this problem, using the above bullet. It makes a fine exit hole!

Ballistics and knockdown power are important when selecting your weapon. Following is a chart of the some of the more common whitetail deer guns/bullets:

Bullet	Ft./Sec. @ 100 Yd.	Trajectory @ 100 Yd.	Ft.-Lb Energy @ 100 Yd.
243 Win w/75 gr. HP	2970	+1.2"	1469
243 Win w/100 gr. BTSP	2728	+1.6"	1653
270 Win w/130 gr. SP	2800	+1.8"	2265
270 Win w/150 gr. SP	2641	+2.1"	2322
7MM Rem Mag w/139 gr. BTSP	2933	+1.2"	2656
7MM Rem Mag w/175 gr. SP	2650	+2.0"	2720
30-30 Win. w/150 gr. RN	1973	0"	1296

30-30 Win. w/170 gr. RN	1895	0"	1355
308 Win. W/150 gr. BTSP	2560	+2.0"	2183
308 Win. W/178 gr. BTHP	2439	+2.5	2351
30-06 w/150 gr. SP	2617	+2.1"	2281
30-06 w/180 gr. BTHP	2695	+2.0"	2902
300 Win Mag w/150 gr. BTSP	2988	+1.2"	2974
300 Win Mag w/190 gr. BTSP	2711	+1.6"	3101

Many people believe that bullets fly in a straight line. This is untrue. They actually travel in a parabolic trajectory or one that becomes more and more curved as range increases and velocity drops off. The projectile actually starts to drop the instant it leaves the firearm's muzzle. However, the centerline of the bore is angled slightly upward in relation to the line of the sights (which are above the bore) so that the projectile crosses the line of sight on its way up (usually around 25 yards or so) and again on its way down at what is called the zero range. Zero Range is the farthest distance at which the line of sight and the projectile's path intersect.

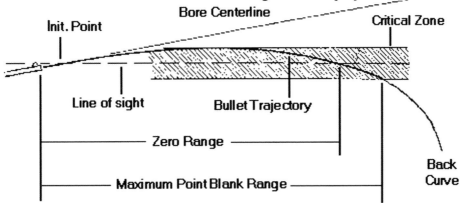

Some hunters use a heavier bullet to minimize bullet deflection, if they were to hit a twig. Personally, I think the only sure cure to bullet deflection is don't hit twigs. Once, I hit a one-forth inch diameter dogwood twig on a thirty-yard shot, using a 30-06, and a one hundred and eighty grain bullet, and it deflected enough to miss the deer. Some hunters use slower bullets because fast ones (especially with a soft point) will explode if they hit a twig. I say "bull". If it didn't explode, it would deflect anyway. You've got to have speed to have accuracy and knockdown energy. I would feel comfortable using any of the above guns/bullets. The important point is to know your gun and its limitations. Like I said above, some hunters place too much emphasis on the gun and not enough on the other ninety-nine percent of important issues necessary to be a skillful whitetail hunter. The ammunition that you choose for your gun is at least equally important to the gun and its sighting device. Manufacturers tailor ammunition to the game by varying the bullet's hardness, shape, jacket, etc. accordingly. Consult the ammunition box, or even the manufacturer, for their recommended ammunition for whitetail. Should I use a sling? Yes! The appropriate deer rifle is rather heavy. It's very nice to let it ride on your shoulder occasionally. Padded slings are OK (unless they get rain soaked) but not necessary; but camouflage is a plus. When your deer target is coming to you, make sure the sling doesn't hang on a limb or something and cost you a kill!

❖ Muzzleloader - Most states have special muzzleloader only hunts. Therefore, most serious whitetail hunters will have a muzzleloader rifle in their rifle inventory. A highly skilled whitetail hunter must select the appropriate muzzleloader for the job. Like guns and bows, there are a lot of good muzzleloaders on the market today. Some hunters prefer the old pioneer version. There is just something about carrying old styles that is appealing to some hunters. Some even use the old flintlock, where you have to wait after you pull the trigger for it to fire, and hope the fine powder, that the flint ignites, isn't too wet to burn. The Thompson muzzleloader is the pioneer style that I see carried most and it does a fine job on most shots. The pioneer styles are less expensive than most in-lines, except for those custom hand made pioneer style muzzleloaders. The biggest disadvantage to them is that they are difficult and time consuming to clean, difficult and time consuming to remove a bullet, and they do not have as much barrel groove twist; therefore, they are not as accurate at a hundred yards as some in-lines. I prefer a stainless steel in-line. They are very accurate, if you choose the correct one. Read the manufacturer's published ballistics to make sure. It should group within an inch and one-half radius at a hundred yards. They are easy to clean and take care of. They are easy to remove a bullet when you forget to put powder in before the bullet or it otherwise fails to fire. They are normally lighter and better balanced, than the pioneer types, for easier carrying. I use a Knight Model MK85 in-line muzzleloader with a Leupold 3x-9x-variablex40 scope and use the large 250 Vorderlader-Zundhutchen percussion cap (No. 1081), during the state muzzleloader hunts.

Muzzleloader caliber? I recommend the fifty caliber. The fifty caliber does the job quite well. It's the most common and therefore easier to find bullets and sabots for it. The forty-five caliber would also work well.

What muzzleloader powder and bullet loading? I'm not going into detail on this. Proper loading must be tailored to a specific muzzleloader. Use the manufacturers recommendation for the type and amount of powder and bullet/sabot. It's safer and your accuracy will probably be better. Using jacketed hollow point bullets with a sabot, rather than the old round balls or even the all-lead hollow point bullet, increases kill power. Anyone who has seen bullets after being fired would agree. The jacketed hollow point flairs much more than other alternatives, giving much more kill power. Also, change the cap at the end of each day during dry weather. During wet weather change it several times each day, unless you are using shotgun caps. Shotgun caps are rather water resistant. Some hunters paint the cap powder with fingernail polish to prevent it from absorbing moisture and becoming soggy on a damp day.

Muzzleloader cleaning - This too must be tailored to a specific muzzleloader and following the manufacturer's recommendations is the best advice. Normally the cleaning process of an inline muzzleloader includes disassemble the muzzleloader into the basic parts. Clean the plug/nipple/bolt and swab the barrel in hot soapy water using a brass brush and then cotton swab or patch. Swab the barrel again with clean water to rinse out the soap. Swab the barrel with dry patches until the patches come out dry and allow the gun to air-dry. Swab the barrel with a patch lightly coated with gun oil, reassemble and store in a dry place. Gun safes with safe heaters are best. When you clean your muzzleloader at the end of a season, do not pour or spray oil down the barrel, as some hunters do. The pooled oil in the chamber can cause a misfire the next time that you use the gun! I personally witnessed a "snap" (cap fires, but the powder didn't ignite) on one of the finest trophies I've seen in the woods because powder was poured in on a pool of oil in the chamber. Further, before you load your muzzleloader the first time, at the beginning the season, fire two to three caps to burn any excess oil from the chamber area.

Muzzleloaders become less and less accurate the more that they are shot without cleaning. This is a VERY IMPORTANT point. Even in the heat of battle the barrel should be swabbed between each shot. In the woods I place a patch in my mouth until moist and then swab the barrel. I do this twice and then use a dry patch before reloading. When swabbing the barrel the first time after shooting, move the ramrod in just a few additional inches on each stroke. If you shove it all the way to the bottom, you may have trouble getting it back out, due to the burned powder buildup inside of the barrel.

❖ Pistols - Handguns, like the bow/crossbow, increase the challenge of hunting the whitetail and allow many disabled hunters to enjoy the sport. Most state laws dictate using a pistol of 0.24 caliber or larger and having a barrel length of four inches or longer. The most accurate and highest energy handguns are long-barreled; bolt action or breakdown single shot chambered for rifle 30-30 shells. Choose this type gun with a 1x-4x-pistol scope and you'll have good accuracy up to seventy-five yards. Use jacketed hollow point, 150 grain, and knockdown energy will be fine. Using this type handgun is not much unlike shooting a 30-30 rifle. Revolvers chambered for pistol cartridges such as 0.454 casull, 0.44 magnum, 0.41 magnum, and the 0.357 magnum can fire several shots without reloading. They are less powerful but will do the job if you know the limitations of the gun and ammunition. A pistol does require much more practice, than a rifle, to become proficient.

❖ Shotgun - Shotguns, using buckshot, are legal in some states in certain circumstances and/or certain counties or areas within the state. In some areas the shotgun using slugs, muzzleloader, and bow are the only legal hunting weapons. I would not recommend using a shotgun for slugs unless the gun is fitted with a slug barrel. If you are shooting a ten or twelve gauge, make sure you use sabot slugs. Full size slugs in the big gauges drop terribly. If I'm hunting a shotgun (slugs) or muzzleloader hunt, I prefer the one shot muzzleloader because of its range and accuracy. Realize that the shotgun is inaccurate and has poor kill power beyond fifty yards. I like the shotgun with buckshot for drive hunting, especially in thick stuff, where forty or fifty yards is as far as you can normally see. Early in my whitetail-hunting career, I killed four nice trophies with twelve-gauge using two and three-quarter inch #4 buckshot. It knocked them down, but they kept getting back up until I had up to the fifth shell unloaded. I was lucky! I should have been using three-inch magnum with at least #1 buckshot and preferably #0 or #00 buckshot. The three and one-half inch chambered shotguns did not exist

93

back then. The disadvantages of the shotgun with buckshot is (1) poor range, (2) illegal in many areas, and (3) deer tend to not bleed well, even with a perfect hit. If you use the shotgun with buckshot, train yourself to keep pulling the trigger until the deer completely stops moving and then shoot one more time! I'm very serious. If it gets out of your sight you may never see it again. Pattern your shotgun at forty yards using #1, #00 and #0 buckshot to see which one your gun shoots the best. Use adjustable sights, and sight it in at forty yards, whether using buckshot or slugs.

❖ Scopes - The choice between using scopes and iron sights is personal preference. When I started wearing bifocal glasses I decided to put scopes on all of my hunting guns. If the target or either of the sights becomes fuzzy, it's time to go to the scope. The switch requires some adjustment time but you'll be glad that you switched. If you choose to use a scope instead of iron sights, pick a reliable one. I think the scope is at least equal in importance to the weapon that it is mounted on. Don't try to cut corners on the scope. I've had cheap scopes fog on the inside on damp days, and once simply turn solid black to look through. This is revolting, especially if you're trying to see a once-a-year target. I recommend not using see-through mounts with a scope. They stand so high it is easy to knock the scope out of position. I used to use them. After I changed to flush mount, I noticed a significant improvement in the way my scope stayed on target. Flip mounts introduce even more inaccuracies than see-through mounts. Some hunters prefer using wide-angle lens, like 3x-9x-variablex50m, but they add weight and bulk to a gun. They also require higher mounts than the traditional 40m scopes, resulting in the scope being easier to knock out of alignment than a more flush type mount.

❖ Sight-in your gun or muzzleloader - Sight in your weapon at the longest distance you will likely shoot when hunting. Most hunters sight in their rifles and muzzleloader rifles at one hundred yards. I sight in at fifty yards, because I seldom have shots over this distance in the terrain that I hunt. Use a gun vice if you have access to one. Otherwise, use a bench-rest with sandbags to brace the gun. Check sight-in on all guns you may carry to the woods at the beginning of each season. Something could have changed. If I can get two out of two shots in a two-inch diameter "bulls eye" at fifty yards I'm happy. Other hunters may say this standard is sloppy. Try to use the same manufacturer's brand and bullet weight in a specific gun all of the time. If you change you should resight your gun. As you can see from the preceding ballistic table, bullet weight can make a difference in how the gun shoots and so can the manufacturing brand of ammunition. You will also find that some manufacturer's brands of ammunition will shoot tighter groupings than others for your gun. When you buy a different gun, you should buy two or three different brands of similar bullet weight and experiment to determine the best for that gun.

❖ Portable Tree Stand - If a whitetail hunter is physically able to use a portable tree stand, it is probably the second most valuable piece of equipment he will use (the most important being the gun/muzzleloader/pistol/bow). If you are a compound bow/crossbow/pistol hunter, where you have to get the deer close for an effective shot, you may be wasting your time if you do not use an elevated stand. If you use deer calling devices, the same is true. I have used eight different stands since I first started hunting from a portable tree stand about twenty years ago, and I feel this makes me somewhat of an expert on the functional objectives of a tree stand. The functional objectives to be met when buying a tree stand are:

➢ Safe going up, coming down, and sitting in the stand. This means it holds to the tree well, it has welded connections, it has a rail around the hunter (unless you are bow hunting), it is sturdy to disallow flexing as the hunter shifts positions, it does not require stepping over something when at hunting height, bottom piece will not dislodge from the tree and leave you stranded up the tree, etc. Capacity rating must be higher than your body weight plus your gear and weapon weight.

➢ Light as possible. Stand weights of the eight that I have used over the years varied from eighteen to thirty-one pounds. Weight becomes more important the further a hunter has to walk in to the hunting spot, and the older you become.

➢ Simple and quick to mount and dismount from the tree. The time required to mount or dismount can vary from less than a minute to near ten minutes.

➢ Quick going up and coming down the tree. Some allow the hunter to take longer steps between bites into the tree than others.

➢ Fit a wide range of tree diameters.

➢ Nests tightly for quiet walking to and from the hunting spot.

➢ Quiet going up and coming down the tree.

➢ Welded joints to prevent popping as the hunter shifts positions.

➢ Has some kind of armrests to help take some pressure off the butt occasionally. Comfortable enough to allow the hunter to stay in the tree for at least four hours.

The stand that I've found that meets these functional objectives best is the Grand Slam Model GS2500M "Magnum" by API Outdoors Inc. and is pictured below. API's Model GS2400 is designed for the bow hunter, having the sit-down climber front bar removed, and it weighs seventeen pounds.

Portable tree stand safety - There are far more hunters hurt and killed from tree stand accidents than being shot. Think about it. A fall from twenty to twenty-five feet (20'-25') could be fatal! Use a safety belt! Even if your stand has a rail around you and you don't have to cross over the seat when you're in the lofty perch, it still isn't OSHA approved. An ounce of prevention is worth a pound of cure, especially when we're talking about our life. Sooner or later you will go to sleep in your tree (probably sooner), have a muscle cramp that bends you double and makes you crazy with pain, have muddy boots slip on the foot platform, etc. Don't take a chance; wear your safety belt! Fasten the safety belt as soon as you reach the elevation that you will sit. Use a belt of thick material so it will not roll up around your waist. If you suddenly became suspended by your belt, the rolled up belt would do more damage than one at full width. I use a three-piece safety belt. One goes around the tree, one goes around me and one is between the two for mobility. The harness types are difficult to strap on in the dark, when your fingers are numb from the cold, and you're wearing four or five layers of clothing, but would be much safer if you ever became suspended. API Outdoors makes one that allows a hunter to strap it on while getting dressed and wear it to the stand. You can wear a coat over it, because the hasp is about head level. I've never been totally suspended by a safety belt, but it has helped me maintain my balance many times. Don't forget that this safety belt doubles for the best drag rope you'll ever find, with a lot less weight to carry around. Make sure your stand is rated for your weight plus gear and weapon weight. Don't climb dead trees. Your tree stand will not bite into the tree as well and a dead limb could come down out of a dead tree. I'm speaking from experience in both cases. Don't climb trees that are leaning significantly. When climbing a leaning tree you must climb on the high side, and if it is leaning too much the stand may spin around to the low side. Trust me, this is a very revolting development. Try to avoid slick bark and scaly bark hickory trees. I took a very quick trip down a slick bark hickory once, and scaly bark hickories are noisy to climb and the climber hangs on the bark. Don't climb when the wind chill is much below thirty degrees Fahrenheit. You'll have to wear so many clothes to stay warm that your mobility is hindered; thus, detrimentally affecting your safety. Don't climb with your weapon slung to your back; rather, use a retriever rope anchored to your stand to pull it up and let it down. If you develop a problem going up or coming down the tree, you will need all of the mobility you can get. I use a little quick snap on the end of my retriever rope to hook to my weapon. They are faster and more secure than a knot, and can be used to hold the rope loops while transporting the stand. If your gun does not have a double safety, remove the chambered round, before going up and coming down the tree. Otherwise, engaging the second safety should be acceptable.

❖ Ground Blinds - Tent type ground blinds of different designs are available. In those cases that I decide to stand hunt on the ground, I normally use two tree umbrellas to create a semicircle around me. I place them between myself and the area I expect the deer to approach. Ideally, I've also got a tree lap, cedar tree, log, or something on one side of me also. Hopefully you're able to find a flat rock or tree trunk to comfortably rest your butt. Most ground blind hunters carry a folding chair or at least a foam cushion to sit on. Remove the leaves in a small area around you, so you will not crunch leaves and twigs as you move or get into shooting position.

❖ Tree Umbrella - Don't laugh, they're fantastic. You can buy them at most any outfitter. They allow you to sit in your tree in a hard rain and remain dry. This is especially important if you forgot to stuff your rain suit in your utility vest before you left your vehicle. They are simple to use. Simply screw the rod into the tree at head height above your tree stand foot platform, open the folded umbrella and set it into the pod at the end of the rod, and tie the strings around the tree. They have a cut-away so they will fit around the tree. If it is likely that a deer under your tree can silhouette you against the sky, consider using a tree umbrella even if you don't expect rain. They make a dandy ground blind too (discussed later). I carry one or two in my utility vest at all times.

❖ Deer Calls - To perform the calls outlined in Chapter Seven, the Hot Doe Breeding Bellow by Woods Wise Products (PO Box 681552-P, Franklin, TN 37068; 800-735-8182), and a buck grunt call with a double reed (like the Knight & Hale EZ-Grunt-er "Plus", Drawer 670, Cadiz, KY; 800-500-9357; http://www.knight-hale.com) is all that you need. Other suppliers of deer calls are: M.A.D. (417-451-4438; outlandsports.com), Primos (601-366-1288; primos.com), and Quaker Boy (800-544-1600; quakerboygamecalls.com). When you select a call, make sure there are clear instructions or an audio tape, so you will be sure that you are making the correct sounds and that your call sequence is correct. Many calls, that I've found, do not include either.

You can also buy electronic calls. Some are expensive but really sound good and simplifies calling. Extreme Dimension makes a digital call and can be located at http://www.phantomcalls.com/gifs/states2.html. Electronic deer calls are illegal to use in at least the following states: CT, FL, GA, ID, KY, MS, NC, NM, PA, RI, SC, SD, UT, and VA and at least parts of CO, DE, IA, KS, and MO. If you plan on hunting a state that you are not familiar with their laws, call the state's Wildlife Agency. Laws tend to change over the years, so be sure that they are legal in your state before buying one.

❖ Vehicle Gear - As do most whitetail hunters, I do most of my hunting within a hundred miles of my house. If I'm hunting within an hour of my house I use my house as "camp". If I hunt over an hour from home, I'll stay in a hotel or at my hunting cabin. In any case my vehicle, and the hunting gear in it, are an important part of my typical hunting day; so, my vehicle must be dependable and well stocked. I make sure that I've got a good spare tire and jack. I carry a few blocks in the bed in case I have to block up to change a tire or to get traction to get out of a mud hole. On the dash I have a barometer mounted for easy view. In the glove box I've got spare fuses, bulbs, and a first aid kit. Behind the seat are: fire extinguisher, toilet tissue, and paper towels. My six-year-old four-wheel drive pickup has a toolbox behind the cab. During whitetail season the toolbox becomes a hunting supply box. My hunting box is stocked with at least the following:

➢ Food box stocked with candies, breakfast bars, canned meats, beans, fruits, etc. and a box of crackers. It's not gourmet but it satisfies my hunger.

➢ Rain gear and spare clothes for unexpected temperature changes.

➢ Hunting satchel stocked with hatchet, hacksaw, knives, garbage bags, scent control bottles, hand warmers and lighter fluid, large six volt light with spare battery, insect repellants, shells (gun season), etc.

➢ An arrow storage and bow accessory box that goes in the hunting box during archery season.

➢ Toolbox with hand tools, wrench set, hammer, nails, duct tape, etc.

Additional items in the bed of the truck include: case of fruit juices, bottled water, tie-down straps to string-up a deer, and a lock and chain to secure a spare portable tree stand and/or at your stand when hunting public areas.

❖ Luxury Equipment - A $50,000 four-wheel drive truck or SUV is nice but not totally necessary. If I can afford such a vehicle and I have other justifications for it (getting to work on time in a snow, hauling stuff on my construction job, etc.), I'll have one – Even if it may be two or three years old when I buy it. Otherwise, I'll just do a little more walking and/or find more accessible places to hunt. I remember hunting a mountain years ago. I took my Jeep Cherokee up a treacherous all big rock and mud road one very early morning to a nice hunting spot. When I finally got there, there set a new Cadillac Eldorado. I did not know, until then, there was a back way in on good roads. Nice vehicles do not make you a skillful whitetail hunter.

ATV's are appropriate, occasionally, to learn what is around the immediate area you are hunting, to travel an old/rough logging road that you do not want to take your new four-wheel drive truck, or to haul a deer out of the woods. If you try to use it to scout the immediate area, that you hunt, you will not see a fraction of what you need to see. In fact, just walking logging roads will also be misleading. You've got to go where the deer will be and deer will not always travel logging roads. If you use ATV's to get to the very end of near impassable roads, you may find that many other hunters on that WMA hunt had the same idea, and a bunch of hunters pile up there and everyone becomes luck hunters. I have a nice Honda 300 ATV, but I seldom use it for hunting purposes. I know a lot of hunters that will "BOO" me for this stand. After a hunter spends $7,000 for the best ATV money can buy, they don't want to leave it at home, when hoofing all over a mountain.

Infrared scouting camera(s) to monitor trails and scrapes may be appropriate. They'll give you a picture of what came down the trail or to a scrape and tell you when it came by. Global positioning system (GPS) hand held units help you maintain your bearings in the woods. I recommend using them if you tend to get "turned around" easily. Sound magnifying devices, if you have a hearing loss, will help you hear a deer before it smells/hears/sees you. Hand held two-way radios. These are nice if you buddy hunt, especially when drive hunting or dog hunting. If you have a serious health problem or physical impairment, it may be a necessity. They may be illegal to use in some areas. Tent-like ground blinds may become important if you can't use a portable tree stand or hunting a spot that has no trees large/straight enough to hang a portable tree stand. Binoculars (light and compact) help you look deep into the woods for movement and deer body parts. They are especially helpful to the still/stalk/boat hunters and/or you do not use a scope. Hand warmers can become the most important equipment that you have on a very cold morning, but I use them as body warmers by placing one in my shirt pocket. They're nice when the wind chill is below thirty degrees Fahrenheit. The above items are mentioned to the reader simply to make sure that you are aware they exist, and none of them are a prerequisite to becoming a highly skilled whitetail hunter.

Cabela's is my outfitter of choice for hard to find hunting gear. Local sporting shops cannot possibly stock what Cabela's can offer in their many catalogues. They offer many brands within a given item. Their catalogue descriptions are very detailed and accurate. To receive free catalogues from them use the following phone number and e-mail address: 1-800-237-4444; www.cabelas.com

Chapter Thirteen
Clothing

Proper clothing will keep you comfortable at your stand in about any weather, and certainly if the wind-chill is above twenty degrees Fahrenheit. There is no reason to be in pain from the cold while sitting at your stand. A whitetail deer hunter needs proper clothing that will keep him/her comfortably warm and dry. You can chill if the temperature is as high as fifty degrees Fahrenheit if you break a sweat walking to your stand, it's a little windy, etc. An uncomfortable hunter will probably move more at their stand, giving the whitetail an advantage that can be avoided. An uncomfortable hunter is less likely to see an approaching deer and will make more mistakes. A terribly uncomfortable hunter may decide that hunting isn't their sport after all.

Purchase clothing that allows dressing in layers and has outerwear texture that will not be noisy, when rubbed against its self. Remember, a deer under your tree can hear cloth rubbing against cloth, as you move into shooting position. I've been there. Soft-flocked pile or wool cloth is much quieter than slick finished cloths. However, the quiet materials will hold more scents than slick cloths, since it has more surface area.

Look for clothing that has scent blocking/neutralizing characteristics, and having camouflage blending with your hunting area.

❖ Utility Belt, Satchel, or Utility Vest? - I prefer a utility vest with a back type game pouch and plenty of pockets. Keeping all of my "to-the-stand" supplies in one place, like my utility vest, ensures that I don't get to my stand and realize that I have forgotten something important. The game pouch can be used to stash: Rain gear; tree umbrella, and limb saw; plastic bag to cover my tree stand seat, in case it rains, when I leave it in the woods, and put my "gut pile" in to get it away from my hunting spot after a kill; carry my coat to/from my stand; and/or booties in low temperatures to place over my boots. It should have four pockets for: Scent control bottles; flashlight and spare set of flashlight batteries; compass; snacks or even lunch if I'm staying all day; lighter for emergencies; rattle bag and deer calls; ammunition; antihistamine to reduce blowing/coughing from a sinus attack; surveyor tape and "bright eyes"; and GPS, two-way radio, binoculars, etc. Long zip-up side pockets are convenient for drink bottles (also used to urinate in when empty) or a small coffee thermos bottle.

Don't let me lead you to believe that you must carry all of these items to become a highly skilled whitetail hunter. Some of the best hunters that I know do not even carry a utility vest. These items are carried by some hunters and are offered to the reader merely as a suggestion. There's nothing wrong with carrying any or all of these items if you are tough enough to hoof them through the woods with your twenty pound tree stand and eight to ten pound shooting device. We've just got to draw the line somewhere. I carry a utility vest most of the time, but I try to keep it as light as possible.

99

Utility Vest

- ❖ Warm Weather Clothing (Above forty-five degree Fahrenheit) – Bow Season (Late September through October)
  - ➢ Hat - Short bill or all around brim is a must to reduce horizontal movement, as seen by the deer. I recommend using military spec "boonie", "Jones" style, or a camouflage baseball cap with a mesh veil attached. Gore-Tex or Dry Plus material for rain protection would be nice.
  - ➢ Boots - All rubber or light duty pac types minimize spreading scent. They are not very comfortable but do keep your feet dry when you get caught in rain or having to wade creeks/swamps/marshes/mud unless your feet sweat badly. In this case you may need to carry an extra set of socks if you plan to do some serious walking.
  - ➢ Socks - Heavy athletes socks work well in temperatures above 45 degrees Fahrenheit if you do not plan on doing much walking. If you plan on serious scouting or still hunting, stay away from cotton socks. Cotton socks absorb sweat, rather than wicking it away from your feet. Once the sock becomes sweat soaked, they begin to slip and slide causing blisters, no matter how good your boots are. For serious walking, wear a pair of polypropylene or acrylic socks as a liner to wick moisture, and cover them with a pair of Thermax, wool, or light wool blend, which continue to wick moisture toward the boot. Now, all you need is a boot that continues to wick the foot moisture and keep external moisture from entering the boot.
  - ➢ Outer wear - The Army fatigues style is hard to beat. They have plenty of pockets, which may reduce the need for carrying a utility vest, if you are walking a mile or so to your stand. If it's a warm day, they are comfortably cool. Some hunters prefer bibs for comfort with a light pullover camouflage knit shirt. A medium duty insulated jacket will be necessary later in bow season in most areas. Rain proof is a plus and it should be of a quiet material. Being scent locking and 3-D would be a definite plus. Your raingear top may work before the weather gets too cold.
  - ➢ Under garments - Silk, silk/wool blend or even polyester/wool blend underwear works well. Satisfy the following functional objectives: wicks body moisture, stretches to body

motions, and lightweight. Some brands advertise to be "scent eliminator" by controlling odor-causing bacteria. A wool sweater may be necessary on cooler morning hunts.

➢ Rain gear - Don't get cheap stuff that may start leaking at seams or "weep" through after a few minutes in a significant rain. This is not the place to cut costs. Get it in a quiet cloth if possible.

➢ Orange vest - Not required or necessary during bow season.

❖ Cold Weather Clothing (Below forty-five degrees Fahrenheit) - Gun Season (November through early January). Dressing in layers is really important during late season hunting, especially if you do some still, driving, or boat hunting during midday.

➢ Hat - I recommend the "Jones" style or the stocking cap (toboggan). I take a green toboggan and an orange one and stitch them together as one. This gives added warmth and allows flexibility to change from orange to green if I want to be less noticeable. Having no bill, it is the least noticeable hat to the deer. In cases where late evening or early morning sun is blinding, I roll the front to create a bill.

➢ Boots - I use two degrees of insulation and both are one size too big for a second pair of heavy socks.
  ■ Cold weather - Heavy insulated "pac" but no liner.
  ■ Extreme Cold - Sorel Dominator "pac", which has a liner and advertises a comfort rating of minus one hundred degrees Fahrenheit. I'm sure this rating assumes the person is walking. My feet stay cozy when sitting on a stand at twenty degrees Fahrenheit wind chill. I don't even have to use "booties" when I wear these. They weigh almost six pounds and the toe ends are rather large and tend to hang on stuff as I walk; therefore, I do not use them unless the temperature dictates doing so.

➢ Socks - Wear a pair of polypropylene or acrylic socks as a liner to wick moisture, and cover them with a pair or two of heavy Thermax or wool blend, which continue to wick moisture toward the boot. The percent wool should be as high as you can find. Don't fall for the battery sock scam. Just when they get the feet sweaty, the battery power will be gone.

➢ Outer wear - Buy one size too big to allow for under garments.
  ■ Pants - A pair of quilted Gore-Tex system (or similar) bibs that comes almost to the armpits is the warmest that I've found. The pair that I use has a layer of Gore-Tex, a layer of Thinsulate LiteLoft insulation, a layer of Scent-Lok, and the outer layer is a quiet type material. They are wind/water proof and breathable. The loose waist allows crotch heat to come up over the body. Some have side zippers that allow the hunter to warm the hands in the crotch area.
  ■ Coat - A Gore-Tex system (or similar) shell with a full goose-down liner gives the most warmth for the weight to carry that I have found. The above system of Gore-Tex, Thinsulate LiteLoft and Scent-Lok would also be a good choice. Find one that comes below the butt to help trap crotch heat and having a quiet material outer layer.

➢ Under garments
  ■ Layer One - Silk, silk/wool blend or even polyester/wool blend underwear works well. It wicks body moisture, stretches to body motions, and is lightweight.
  ■ Layer Two - I suggest two-piece goose down underwear. Don't forget that down comes in different qualities. The label should read Northern Goose down and loft (fluff) to about five hundred and fifty cubic inches per ounce. The fluffier it is, the more trapped air you have around your body, and the better insulated you are from the cold.

- ■ Layer Three - A quilted shirt gives a pocket to carry a hand warmer if it really gets cold.
- ■ Layer Four - Use a goose down vest. This probably will not be necessary for most hunters, unless you are sitting for long hours at below twenty degrees Fahrenheit wind chill.
- ➢ Rain gear - Even if your cold weather outerwear has a Gore-Tex or equal layer, you'll need to keep a good rain suit available. Rainproof outerwear will keep you dry but, since it has a heavy outer layer that absorbs water, it will become very heavy after being in a significant rain for a while. If you use a tree umbrella at your stand, such outerwear should be all you need if you do not have a long walk to and from your stand. If you still and/or drive hunt you'll definitely need a good rain suit in your utility vest. The same rain suit you use in bow season (described above) should work nicely.
- ➢ Gloves - Use Gore-Tex/Thinsulate quilted glove/mitten for below freezing. I wear this on my left hand and keep my right hand in my pocket (or crotch if it's real cold) so I can shoot easily. Some hunters use a similar glove on both hands but with a door that allows the fingers to come out. Use military knit wool gloves for above freezing. Use two gloves on one hand if necessary. This satisfies my needs in most weather.
- ➢ Scarf - A very thick military type wool scarf holds in body heat. I keep one in my coat pocket at all times.
- ➢ Boot "booties" - These are quilted with a zipper down the back. Pull them in over your boots when you get to your stand (or your feet get cold at your stand) and you can handle twenty degree Fahrenheit wind chill. Some will fold flat and be easy to carry in a utility vest.
- ➢ Orange vest - The purpose of wearing orange in the woods is to avoid getting shot by other hunters. State laws require this during gun seasons. The state hunting laws also dictate how many square inches of orange we must wear. My state requires "five hundred square inches of daylight fluorescent orange". Regardless of the law, I would choose to wear one, especially if hunting where there're other hunters in the area. Vests are more flexible than using an orange coat or coveralls. Regardless of what you need to wear on a given day, you can put it in over the last layer and be safe and legal. Some hunters pull them off once at their stand. If a hunter chooses the right cloth and washes it in no brightener detergent, they shouldn't tell much difference in how easily a deer detects them. Use cloth, not plastic. Plastic tears easily when cold, reflects light more than cloth, and is noisy. Try to find one with a texture that doesn't reflect light. A deer can't see colors but some fabrics/colors reflect light more than others. Try to find one that has a game pouch and utility pockets so it's more than just a safety vest. Some still hunters use all orange coveralls. When walking, warmth is not as important as when stand hunting. If you prefer this, you should use camouflage orange.

Cabela's is my outfitter of choice for clothing, as it is with hard to find specialty equipment mentioned earlier, and for the same reasons.

Chapter Fourteen
Whitetail Hunting Safety

All states, that I am aware of, require hunters born before a certain date to complete a Mandatory Hunter Education course, which includes safety; thus, this book does not focus on safety. However, it is my moral duty as a writer to dedicate space in this book to this very important part of whitetail hunting.

There are far more hunters hurt and killed from tree stand accidents than from being shot. As outlined in Chapter Five under "Permanent Tree Stands", I strongly discourage using permanent tree stands. Not only are they unsafe, they are inflexible. Please reread Chapter Eleven under "Portable Tree Stand", Portable tree stand safety". I stated in Chapter Eleven that portable tree stands are "probably the second most valuable piece of equipment" a hunter will use. However, regardless of how much more successful they make you as a whitetail hunter, their use is not worth a major injury or death.

Alcohol/drugs and hunting of any kind do not mix! We have strict laws prohibiting drinking and driving, and stiff penalties to enforce these laws. Isn't it at least equally dangerous to carry a firearm as to be driving, while under the influence of alcohol/drugs? If you see fellow hunters using alcohol/drugs in or around your hunting area, I strongly recommend that you relocate to another area. In this case, especially if you are hunting in a Wildlife Management Area, isn't it your civic duty to report such hunters to a law officer?

Parents, don't unleash your thirteen year old on the rest of us hunters, without your supervision. The Mandatory Hunter Education course is great, but it doesn't miraculously bestow instant good judgment to a teenager. Good judgment only comes with time and continued supervision from us adults. Being with your teenagers in the woods is a perfect opportunity for some painless/natural bonding/training that our teenagers desperately need these days, when their peers seem to have more influence than we parents. What better opportunity could parents have to discuss morals, values, drugs/alcohol, etc. than while enjoying each other's companionship on a hunting trip?

The bullet fired from a whitetail-hunting rifle has no conscience. It can kill any living thing that it hits, for miles, without having any remorse. Before you go to your stand, know where any residences are within at least a mile of your stand. Before you squeeze the trigger, know that your bullet is under control. Another big advantage of hunting from a portable tree stand is that the angle, that you normally shoot, is toward the ground, and the ground is probably the safest possible backstop for your unremorseful bullet. Remember, you are responsible for your bullet, even if it hits something or someone two miles away. How would you like to live with the knowledge that your bullet killed someone, or even some farmer's cow?

Avoid getting lost. Although I cannot speak from experience, I'm sure spending a night in the wilderness in below freezing temperatures may be worse than a revolting development. Chapter Six, under "Keeping Your Bearings", outlines ways to prevent a hunter from becoming confused and getting turned around in the woods. Some people have more of a problem with maintaining bearings in the woods than others. If you have a problem maintaining your bearings in the woods, I strongly recommend that you invest in a global positioning system device (GPS), as detailed in Chapter Six, and a spare set of batteries for it. When you are tracking a wounded deer and you are excited about the possible/probable kill, you can find yourself out of familiar territory. I never worried about this as long as I had plenty of daylight left. But, if nightfall is coming in this scenario, a hunter can panic and make poor judgment decisions. I'm sure a GPS in this situation could quickly become the most important piece of equipment the hunter has with him.

Learn the difference between the sounds that a hunter makes, walking through the leaves, compared to the sound of a deer or other animal. This could reduce the possibility of shooting a fellow hunter. Wear your daylight fluorescent orange and don't be tempted to remove it when you get to your stand.

When drive hunting, the driver(s), if not the stander(s) too, should wear head-to-toe daylight fluorescent orange. Also, when drive hunting, have a plan for each drive and make sure that all hunters know the plan. Make sure that the stander(s) know roughly where the driver(s) will exit the driven area.

Respect the poisonous snakes, especially when walking to your morning stand and away from your evening stand in the dark. Poisonous snakes are more of a problem in some areas than others. They are also more of a problem early in the season, before the temperature drives them into hibernation. If you are hunting in an area known to have a significant poisonous snake population, and it has not been cold enough to drive them into hibernation, I recommend that you invest in a good pair of snake boots or snake leggings.

Chapter Fifteen
Persistence

Even after learning what I have tried to teach you in this book, as well as how to apply what you learned, don't expect to kill a whitetail deer every time that you go in the woods. It just doesn't work that way. Most young hunters, that I've taken whitetail hunting, seemed to expect deer to behave like those in a fenced wildlife park or a petting zoo. At the end of the first hour of hunting, one such youngster said in a loud voice, "There's no deer here", and one snorted behind us and ran. A fisherman must keep his bait in the water if he expects to catch fish. Hunting for the whitetail is no different. Hunting for a trophy whitetail requires considerably more patience and persistence than does hunting for any legal deer. About one out of 2.2 hunters, buying a whitetail permit, fills a tag, buck or doe. Learning what this book has to teach you and then learning to apply the knowledge will dramatically improve these odds. This book was written with the primary objective of making you a highly skilled whitetail hunter, but you've got to spend time in the whitetail woods to make this happen.

Even after you have learned every point, that I have tried to teach you, and how to apply them, you'll make mistakes, but you will also bring home more meat and trophies. Don't be too rough on yourself for making mistakes. Rather, realize what you did wrong and correct it in the future. For example, if your tree stand, with bolted joints, pops when your moving into shooting position and your trophy bolts and runs, get rid of it and purchase one that accomplishes all functional objectives, outlined in Chapter Eleven under "Portable Tree Stands". I once spent two years (off and on) hunting for a buck that was horning two-inch oaks and ripping them off near the ground. I never so much as saw the buck. Another time I had found similar sign, I went to sleep in my tree stand, and woke up to what sounded like someone running off the side of the mountain with an eight-foot two-by-four strapped to their chest. Still another time I saw, out of the corner of my eye, a nice buck coming over the crest of a hill to my left. As I shifted my body to get into shooting position (it was bow season), my bolted together tree stand popped and there went my opportunity for a trophy. I could go on and on about bucks that I almost got. Any experienced whitetail hunter could. This is part of what makes hunting the whitetail so intriguing and exciting. If it were easy it would remove the challenge, and therefore fun, from the sport.

If you are willing to spend long hours in the woods scouting for the perfect stand, sit for three or four hours at your stand in the morning and evening or all day (even when you get a little cold), dedicate days or weeks each year to hunting the whitetail, and apply the principles in this book, you will kill deer. Occasionally, you will kill a trophy. More importantly, if you love being in the woods, matching your wits with the instincts of a shrewd old buck, you will have experiences that you will keep the rest of your life, and you would not trade them for anything.

A normal meat hunter will only have one or two opportunities per season to kill a trophy. A serious and experienced buck hunter, that knows what he is doing and spends a lot of time in the woods, may only have three or four opportunities per season for a trophy. The more you learn, the more you apply your knowledge, the more time you spend in the woods, the better your equipment and clothing, etc., the better your odds become of bringing home meat/trophies.

Most sports are team oriented and if your team wins/succeeds, you're seldom sure how much, if anything, that you contributed to the team efforts. Excluding drive hunting, whitetail hunting is a one-on-one sport – your wits vs. the whitetail's instincts. When you plan your strategy, follow through and kill a nice buck, there's no question that you made it happen.

Consider getting your spouse, girlfriend/boyfriend involved in hunting with you. It's a great opportunity to do some serious "bonding". If you have a son or daughter, take them to your state's Mandatory Hunter Education course. Take them on your state's juvenile hunts and spend time in the woods with them. What better opportunity could a parent have to teach their kids the morals, values, and principles a child desperately needs to learn? What better tool could you find than this book, *SKILLFULLY HUNTING THE ELUSIVE WHITETAIL*, to teach your kids, spouse, girlfriend/boyfriend or friend how to hunt skillfully. What better example could you be than following the state hunting laws?

If you know whitetail hunters who have hunted for years, killing few or no deer, introduce them to this book. It could be that they will quit hunting all together, out of the frustration of being unsuccessful. Similarly, if you know someone who totally quit whitetail hunting, introduce him or her to this book. It could be they quit out of frustration of not seeing deer in the woods. The art of hunting the whitetail, or any other game, can be learned like any other art. It's not a simple art, but it's not a rocket science either.

As time passes, from one hunting season to another, you'll forget some of the fine points that I've tried to teach you in this book, maybe remembering some point or two, after you've made the mistake again. Consider rereading this book at the beginning of each new hunting season. Even though I wrote the book, I'll forget some points also. So, I plan to reread this book at the beginning of each deer-hunting season. This is one reason that I decided to write the book.